*THOUGHTS TO TAKE HOME
FOR LENT*

*FROM THE THREE CYCLES
OF LENTEN READINGS*

THOUGHTS TO TAKE HOME FOR LENT

FROM THE THREE CYCLES OF LENTEN READINGS

by Mujana Darian

FRANCISCAN HERALD PRESS
Chicago, Illinois 60609

Thoughts To Take Home For Lent, From the Three Cycles of Lenten Readings, by Mujana Darian. Copyright © 1973 by Franciscan Herald Press, 1434 West 51st Street, Chicago, Illinois 60609. Library of Congress Cataloging in Publication Data: BX2170.L4D37   242'.34   73-2619 ISBN 0-8199-0452-X. Made in the United States of America.

~~~~~~~~~~~~~~~~~~~~~~~~~

NIHIL OBSTAT:
 Marion A. Habig O.F.M.
 Censor Deputatus

IMPRIMATUR:
 Msgr. Richard A. Rosemeyer, J.C.D.
 Vicar General, Archdiocese of Chicago

February 12, 1973
CHICAGO, ILLINOIS

The Scripture had been quoted
from the NEW AMERICAN BIBLE.

"*The Nihil Obstat and the Imprimatur are official declarations that a book or pamphlet is free of doctrinal or moral error. No implication is contained therein that those who have granted the Nihil Obstat and Imprimatur agree with the contents, opinions, or statements expressed.*"

FOREWORD

"God, who at sundry times in divers manners spoke" (Heb. 1: 1), speaks to us in a special way at holy Mass. Augustin Leonard in his *Toward a Theology of the Word of God* says: "Our age seems to have been given the grace to begin anew to listen with greater attention to the living and efficacious Word of God."

One of this new type of listeners is Mujana Darian. She felt from the time of her conversion (from Protestantism as a teenager) the need to take something home with her from Mass. Since there was seldom a homily during the weekday Mass she started inventing her own commentaries; she brought home her own message to put into practice during the day. This led to the book, *Thoughts to Take Home for Advent* and now *Thoughts to Take Home for Lent*. Her interpretations are not based on exegetical commentaries, but are prompted by her own personal immediate reactions to the unstudied word. They are quite original, fresh, and sometimes surprising, and always down to earth. It has nothing to recommend it but its entire simplicity, and as St. Paul says of his own teaching, "It has none of the persuasive force of 'wise' argumentation, but the convincing power of the Spirit. So that your faith rests not on the wisdom of men, but on the power of God" (1 Cor. 2: 4-5).

The author depends heavily upon "the power of God." She does not skimp on prayer and suffering as the source of God's blessing on her work. Daily Mass and the full divine office of the clergy, and living with a lively sense of the presence of God have been her practices for many years.

The "Thoughts to Take Home" take a phrase from the Scripture Reading for the Mass of the day and put it into modern dress for modern living. On Ash Wednesday the warning of Jesus about being "on guard against performing acts for people to see" is put in a familiar setting by the now popular TV expression *"What you see is what you get."* (If you do things merely for man to see you have already received all the reward you are going to get.) And when Jesus reminds us to take up our cross and follow

Him, the "Thoughts" remind us that "as Jesus' cross came from man, so does ours come from man," and she chides, *"Isn't it amazing how we think we can handle a 'big cross' when we grumble and carry on while carrying the little ones?"* When Lenten sacrifices make you grumpy, she suggests that you *"sacrifice your sacrifice and make being-cheerful be your sacrifice."* For "fasting that makes you *disagreeable* to all around you certainly will not make you *agreeable to God."*

This book can put the faithful in the pew and the priest at the altar on the same wavelength. The Mass-goer comes from home out of the busy work-a-day world with his mind full of practical material needs of the day. The priest comes from his study filled with the meaning of the day's liturgy, ready to soar high into the sky of his homily . . . and "ne'er the twain shall meet." But they can meet if both layman and priest first take a look at *Thoughts to Take Home for Lent.* It will bring the priest out of the clouds and the layman will find the "Thoughts" like yeast in the dough of his liturgy participation. It will start things rising. He will be drawn into the habit of listening to the Mass readings with initiative and originality. And when he leaves church he *will* have "thoughts to take home" with him.

VALERIAN SCHOTT O.F.M.

CONTENTS

Foreword v

Introduction ix

Ash Wednesday 3
    Thursday after Ash Wednesday 6
    Friday after Ash Wednesday 8
    Saturday after Ash Wednesday 10

First Sunday of Lent 12
    Monday of the 1st Week of Lent 21
    Tuesday of the 1st Week of Lent 23
    Wednesday of the 1st Week of Lent 25
    Thursday of the 1st Week of Lent 27
    Friday of the 1st Week of Lent 29
    Saturday of the 1st Week of Lent 31

2nd Sunday of Lent 33
    Monday of the 2nd Week of Lent 42
    Tuesday of the 2nd Week of Lent 44
    Wednesday of the 2nd Week of Lent 46
    Thursday of the 2nd Week of Lent 48
    Friday of the 2nd Week of Lent 50
    Saturday of the 2nd Week of Lent 52

3rd Sunday of Lent 54
    Optional Mass, the 3rd Week of Lent 63
    Monday of the 3rd Week of Lent 65
    Tuesday of the 3rd Week of Lent 67
    Wednesday of the 3rd Week of Lent 69
    Thursday of the 3rd Week of Lent 71
    Friday of the 3rd Week of Lent 73
    Saturday of the 3rd Week of Lent 75

4th Sunday of Lent 77
    Optional Mass, the 4th Week of Lent 85
    Monday of the 4th Week of Lent 88
    Tuesday of the 4th Week of Lent 90
    Wednesday of the 4th Week of Lent 92
    Thursday of the 4th Week of Lent 94
    Friday of the 4th Week of Lent 96
    Saturday of the 4th Week of Lent 98

5th Sunday of Lent 100
   Optional Mass, the 5th Week of Lent 109
   Monday of the 5th Week of Lent 111
   Tuesday of the 5th Week of Lent 114
   Wednesday of the 5th Week of Lent 116
   Thursday of the 5th Week of Lent 118
   Friday of the 5th Week of Lent 120
   Saturday of the 5th Week of Lent 122

Passion Sunday (Palm Sunday) 124
   Monday of Holy Week 131
   Tuesday of Holy Week 133
   Wednesday of Holy Week 135
   Holy Thursday 137
   Good Friday 140
   Easter Vigil 143

Easter Sunday 147

Chair of St. Peter, Apostle (Febr. 22) 151

St. Joseph, Husband of Mary 153

Annunciation of Our Lord 156

Index 159

INTRODUCTION

We live in a time when everyone wants to have a fast "take-off." We want to get the facts quick. And we do not want to be *bogged down* with a whole lot of details. Most of us have gotten off on the wrong foot concerning Scripture at Mass. We think it is just something the priest talks about in a sermon on Sunday. And *if there is any message* for us we expect the priest to "sledge-hammer" it into us . . . which he does quite skillfully at times. But much too often we have wrapped ourselves in an impenetrable covering of worldly affairs that defies all his efforts. And the less we learn, the louder we holler about *not getting anything out of Mass.* And the tighter we secure our blinders, the more we are convinced of our opinion that there are no thoughts to take home. *The priest just did not get through to us!* He is to blame! No, the priest is not to blame; we are. The priest's sermon is *a preparation for God to speak to us* AFTER WE LEAVE MASS. Oh, there are times when we are lost in a confusion and profusion of words, and the distance between the Scripture messages as-they-ought-to-be and as-they-are is very great. But with a little more attentiveness to the Readings themselves, the bridge can be gapped if we *really want a message to come across.*

This book has been written with the hope that you who read it will discover how simple it is to pinpoint some message from God each day at Mass. It is short and to the point. There is no fanfare, no scholarly exegesis type of lesson, and certainly not what one would call a high-level type of spiritual aid. It deals with simple but perplexing things that come into our everyday living . . . like anger, forgiveness, love, death, hate, sickness, etc., and even how we unknowingly betray our Lord. These are simply the thoughts I took home from Mass during the Lenten Season. I sincerely hope that they will be of help to you during this Lent.

M. D.

*THOUGHTS TO TAKE HOME
FOR LENT*

*FROM THE THREE CYCLES
OF LENTEN READINGS*

Ash Wednesday #220

READING 1

"Blow the Trumpet in Zion! Proclaim a Fast . . ." (Jl. 2: 12-18).

Thought

Proclaiming a fast does not gain you any *merit* unless you plan on *keeping the fast.*

Fasting and sacrificing during Lent has not gone "out of style" or been *eliminated*. The Church, realizing your maturity, has left it up to you to willingly choose your own penance. The main topic of Lent *used to be* what we were going to "give up" for Lent. Of course, many times it was just *a topic*. We never really got around to doing everything or even anything we proclaimed to want to do; our spirit was willing but our flesh was weak. Our grandiose plans were so out of proportion to our ability to keep them that we felt defeated before we even started.

Application

This year make just one intention *of sacrifice. If you can do more . . . this is fine . . . but concentrate on* keeping the one *to the best of your ability. Every hardship and inconvenience that you undergo because of your devotion to God, will be more than compensated for in Heaven.*

Ash Wednesday #220

READING 2

"We are Ambassadors for Christ . . ." (2 Cor. 5: 20, 6: 2).

Thought

One gets to *know Christ* by how His *ambassadors act*.

An ambassador is one who visits somebody or some place as a representative of the highest authority of another country. He has to put aside his own personal feelings and carry out the will of the one he represents. And so it should be with our ambassadorship for Christ. *Our own personal likes and dislikes toward another have nothing to do with our carrying out His will.* In fact, the more effort it costs us to overcome our own will, the more grace we will receive for doing it.

Application

There may be some people who just do not "set well" with you; your personalities clash. The fact that they "irk" you gives you an opportunity to prove your ambassadorship for Christ. *Set aside your own feelings and be kind and friendly towards them.*

Ash Wednesday #220

GOSPEL

"Be on Guard against Performing Religious Acts for People to See . . ." (Mt. 6: 1-6, 16-18).

Thought

An act performed *just to gain attention* is no doubt one of *the devil's inventions.*

It is a natural inclination for us to do things for others to observe; it gives us an incentive. But there are some who thrive on attention and expect credit for their every performance. If there is no audience looking on, there is no performance! There is nothing wrong in getting credit for things we do, but to merely perform a religious act for the sole purpose of having others note how holy you are, is the wrong motive. Like one of the TV performers says: "What you see is what you get!" and that is a good description of how much reward you will get. The *attention of man* that you wanted to receive on earth *is all you will receive.*

Application

Let the attention of God *be your motive for practicing your Faith. If you are observed while going to Mass, saying the rosary, saying meal prayers, etc., that is fine. But do not* seek to be observed *as your purpose for doing them. Be constant in your acts of worship, with or without an audience!*

Thursday after Ash Wednesday #221

READING 1

"The Blessing and the Curse . . ." (Dt. 30: 15-20)

Thought

Anything can become a blessing or a curse . . . according to *how we use it.*

Nothing that we have or use is good or evil of itself. It becomes a blessing or a curse according to which way we choose to make it. A drink is certainly a blessing when we are thirsty, but a curse when we let over-indulgence wipe out our sense of reasoning. Money is a blessing, but when we let the covetous desire for it become our main goal in life it becomes a curse. Storms of temptation appear to be a curse, but if we resist them they become a blessing. Disasters seem to be a curse, but if we turn more fervently to God in prayer they become a blessing.

Application

God used joyful things as well as adversity to carry out His plan. Of course, if we have our choice, we prefer the joyful things. Yet we see that Jesus used what we would certainly term as a curse . . . crucifixion . . . to carry out his plan to save all mankind. He made a curse become a blessing for us. You also, by your free will, have a choice. Try to make the best out of all the events in your life. The blessing and the curse both have a purpose. Use them all to draw you closer to God.

Thursday after Ash Wednesday #221

GOSPEL

"Whoever Wishes to Be My Follower Must Deny His Very Self, Take Up His Cross Each Day . . ." (Lk. 9: 22-25).

Thought

You can't carry your cross *until you pick it up.*

Crosses are there *everyday* for you to "take up." Too often you overlook the crosses of small inconveniences that plague your day. (You're going to work and the tire is flat. The house isn't straightened and unexpected company arrives. The neighbor is sick and you have to spend the day there instead of shopping. You have to put up with daily calls from an elderly aunt. Etc.) You are so busy searching for the big things to please God . . . the main beam of the cross . . . that you do not realize that it takes the *little nails of inconveniences to fasten you there.* And isn't it amazing how we think we can handle a "big cross" when we grumble and carry on while carrying the little ones?

Application

One of the problems is we do not expect our crosses to come through man . . . *but nevertheless, they do. The cross of Jesus came through man. Why should we expect ours to be different? When difficulties and hardships that can't be avoided come through man, don't complain. Accept them cheerfully, calling to mind that this is your* small *way of sharing the cross and a way to prove and strengthen your love of God . . . and man.*

Friday after Ash Wednesday #222

READING 1

"Yes, Your Fast Ends in Quarreling and Fighting . . ." (Is. 58: 1-9).

Thought

Fasting that makes you *disagreeable* to all around you certainly will not make you *agreeable to God.*

We all know some people who have gone on a diet or given up smoking. They have become so disagreeable we wish they would give up "giving up" and get back to their cheerful disposition. And some of them did not have too agreeable a disposition to start with! They never really succeed with their sacrificing mainly because they have never given their whole-hearted consent. Fasting or sacrificing for God is like that also. Unless we really *give our whole-hearted consent* . . . expecting and preparing for some trying moments . . . we will not succeed either. We will end up like Holy Scripture says: "quarreling and fighting, striking with wicked claw" (v.4).

Application

Be considerate of others with your fasting and sacrificing. If you find yourself . . . or others find you . . . "out of sorts," then sacrifice your sacrifice *and make being cheerful or being more agreeable your penance. Choose something else like attending Mass more often or saying the rosary.*

Friday after Ash Wednesday #222

GOSPEL

"John's Disciples Came to Him With the Objection, 'Why Is It That While We . . . Fast, Your Disciples Do Not?' . . ." (Mt. 9: 14-15).

Thought

An objection is often times *a jealous complaint.*

An objection should express disapproval of some one's conduct, with the purpose of *helping* him not *condemning* him. But many times, like the Pharisees, when we make an objection it is not so much because we are disapproving of what some one else is doing, as it is that we are envious and jealous. We are really disapproving *because he is getting to do something and we are not!* And for some reason that does not set too well with us. In our envy we are completely overlooking how much more merit we might be gaining by sacrificing more. Of course, the other fellow's sacrifice or non-sacrificing is really none of our business. He has to make his own choice according to the dictates of his conscience.

Application

We reveal our unloving spirit by our attitude of contempt and caustic criticism of others. Be more charitable. Do not be so quick to judge whether some one else is doing his part for Lent. Be more concerned about doing your part.

Saturday after Ash Wednesday   #223

READING 1

"Seeking Your Own Interests . . ." (Is. 58: 9-14).

Thought

Seeking your own interest is all right as long as *your interest leads you closer to God.*

We hear so much these days about the importance of "self-fulfillment." It is supposed to give us a well-rounded life and a sense of satisfaction. But unfortunately most of the time "self-fulfillment" does just exactly what is says. It fills man so much with "self" that *there is not much room left for God!* A life without God, for whom your life was made, can only end in an eventual feeling of desolation. Seeking your own interests is all right as long as *your ultimate goal is God.* A God-oriented life does not mean one that has you on your knees all the time. Or one that excludes all the things that interest you. God gave you this wonderful world to enjoy. If you do not have an enthusiastic interest in it you would be failing to appreciate that which He has given to you.

Application

Pursue your interests but if you find they begin to exclude God . . . keeping you from Mass . . . then give them up or moderate them. No amount of temporary so-called enjoyment is worth a permanent punishment of being separated from God.

Saturday after Ash Wednesday #223

GOSPEL

"Why Do You Eat and Drink With Tax Collectors and Non-Observers of the Law?" (Lk. 5: 27-32).

Thought

We can't expect "non-observers of the law" to improve if they *never have a reason to improve.*

When the tax collectors or anyone else repented Jesus did not elaborate or dwell upon the horrors of their wickedness. He stressed their repentance and sent them away in peace. By His example and that of His followers *He gave reason* for a sinner *to want to change.* How differently we do things. Our tendency is to hang on, to harp and keep bringing up some one's sinful past. Or if we manage to keep silent about it, we wait with anxious breath, wondering just when he will "pull something" again.

Application

When a person shows a desire to do better, your confidence can go a long way to encourage him. Trust him and let him know it. It will give him strength in time of temptation. Consider how you would feel under the same circumstances and act accordingly.

First Sunday of Lent, Cycle A   #22

READING 1

"DESIRABLE FOR GAINING WISDOM . . ." (Gn. 2: 7-9, 3: 1-7).

THOUGHT

Man would be better off if he *remained ignorant of some of the knowledge* he desires to gain.

It is said . . . "The things we *know* don't usually frighten us." But, judging by the result of today's knowledge (as well as in the time of Adam and Eve), maybe *it should frighten us.* Certainly not all knowledge leads us to wisdom. An uncontrolled desire to attain knowledge can be dangerous. It can be a source of temptation. Like a fly investigating a spider web, we think we can get involved and still remain aloof. We think we can withdraw at will, but meanwhile the web of sin has entangled and encircled us so that there is no escape.

APPLICATION

It is not necessary to take drugs to see if it will destroy your mind, or to touch a high voltage wire to see if it has 20,000 volts in it. Knowledge of some things is not necessarily wisdom. *If your seeking of knowledge runs the risk of drawing you away from God, it is better left alone.*

First Sunday of Lent, Cycle A #22

READING 2

"A Single Offense Brought Condemnation . . . A Single Righteous Act Brought . . . Acquittal . . ." (Rom. 5: 12-19).

Thought

Our concern should not be so much with the "sin" Adam and Eve *brought upon us* as the "redemption" Christ *brought for us.*

Worrying and being overly concerned about confessed sins of the past is useless . . . like trying to do something about the air that used to be in our tire before we had a flat. If you are truly sorry about them, let them go. Do what you can to make amendment but don't dwell upon them. Because of our own unforgiving tendencies and sinfulness, sometimes we find it hard to believe that we can approach God and find complete acceptance from Him. Jesus has already attained and fulfilled the requirements for us so that we have the great privilege of direct access to Heaven. He has already borne our trials and carried our sorrows. Being truly man *He knows the heavy crushing weight of them* to weak and sinful man. He did not do all these things to have us living unhappily, always shamefully looking back to past sins. He wants us to look joyfully, hopefully to what lies ahead . . . Heaven.

Application

We cannot change the past but we can leave it behind. *A sin in your past life should not becloud all the rest of what lies ahead. Use the memory of it to remind you to forgive others as thoroughly as God has forgiven you.*

First Sunday of Lent, Cycle A   #22

GOSPEL

"Jesus Was Led Into the Desert By the Spirit to Be Tempted By the Devil" (Mt. 4: 1-11).

Thought

Being *led* some place to be tempted does not mean we have to *give in* to the temptation.

You might be surprised that the Spirit would lead Jesus into the desert to be tempted by the devil. He had His reasons. He submitted to these attacks in order to show us that *temptation in itself is not sinful.* It can be a challenge; a chance to prove our faith or a chance to show how weak we are. And just as a pirate does not bother to attack an empty ship or one with worthless cargo, the devil doesn't bother that kind of a person either. He attacks those loaded with a valuable cargo of virtue; those whom he fears may elude him or draw others closer to God. *Temptation is sometimes necessary to settle us and confirm us in our spiritual life* . . . like the winds that cause the mighty cedars to dig deeper into the soil of the mountains. Root yourself firmly in your Faith and nothing can uproot you.

Application

Recognize temptation for what it is; a challenge, a chance to draw you closer to God. Do not be troubled by it. You can turn away. *God never allows you to be tried beyond what you can stand.*

First Sunday of Lent, Cycle B #23

READING 1

"I Will Recall the Covenant I Have Made . . ."
(Gn. 9: 8-15).

Thought

If we thought God remembered His "covenant" *in the same degree we remember ours,* we wouldn't have much faith.

All throughout the Bible we see that God has never broken His covenant with mankind. But still some have turned away and refused to accept it. A covenant . . . a promise . . . is a solemn agreement of fellowship and faith that binds two parties by a contract. It is something that is made *willingly,* not by *force.* And once made we cannot readily be excused from it. We *expect* promises made by others with us to be kept. We are apt to carry on if they renege even a little bit. Of course, as for ourselves, we can find many excuses why we do not have to *keep ours.* With so many broken promises of man, it is good that we do not judge God's promises *by our standards;* we would have no faith at all.

Application

Do not be so quick to make rash promises. Consider whether or not you can really keep them. If you feel you cannot, have the honesty to say so. A promise involves more than words on your lips. It binds you to a contract of fulfillment.

First Sunday of Lent, Cycle B #23

READING 2

"The Pledge to God of an Irreproachable Conscience . . ." (1 Pt. 3: 18-22).

Thought

An irreproachable conscience is one that places your actions *beyond reproach of God and man* . . . not one that places your actions *beyond the reproach of your conscience.*

The conscience is a moral strength . . . a natural law . . . placed in the heart by God that helps determine right and wrong. No one can plead ignorance of it. No education is needed. Even a small child who cannot read or speak any words, feels uncomfortable, frightened, or ashamed when he has done something wrong. A man driving along . . . speeding . . . *knows* he is breaking the law. He keeps his eye peeled for radar or the patrol car. And he is not really too surprised if he gets caught. His inner feelings have already warned him. The first time a person misses Mass, regardless of the reason . . . even sickness . . . he feels quite bad about it; he just can't rest easy. And even the second or third time might bother a bit . . . but the sharp edge is gone and he can give himself an excuse and seems justified by it. But eventually he has no qualms at all about missing Mass. His actions have been stretched beyond the reproach of his conscience.

Application

Pay heed to your conscience. If you ignore this warning often enough you begin to lose all sense of God's values *and let the* devil's values "take over."

First Sunday of Lent, Cycle B #23

GOSPEL

"Put to the Test There By Satan . . ." (Mk. 1: 12-15).

Thought

"Put to the test" reminds us that *we have a part* in determining the outcome.

Being "put to the test" with storms of temptation may appear cruel, but does it not give more intense earnestness to our prayers? During those times *we really know we need God.* Temptation often comes upon a person with its strongest power when he is nearest to God. The devil aims high. After all he got one apostle to say *he did not even know Jesus!* And another to sell out our Lord for thirty pieces of silver! We would like to think of the devil as a superstition or a bugaboo used to scare little children. He would like for us to think that too. But he is a *reality* with plenty years of experience. He strikes again and again. If one method does not work, he resorts to another. Temptation even appears as innocent suggestions that cover up deep insidious actions. He glosses over the badness of something by enlarging the appeal of goodness that can be obtained by evil ways. His disguises are endless.

Application

Whatever in your life you have not given to God the devil will try to claim at the earliest opportunity. If you yield nothing of yourself to the devil he can have no hold on you. At the first sign of temptation . . . pray. Pray hard until you get your mind off of the temptation. *Say short prayers often during the day asking God for strength.*

First Sunday of Lent, Cycle C #24

READING 1

"WE CRIED TO THE LORD . . ." (Dt. 26: 4-10).

THOUGHT

There is a *big difference* between "crying about" the things we need and "crying out" our needs to the Lord.

God places *what we need first,* whereas we place *what we want first.* With distracting anxiety and worry the biggest bulk of our effort and thought seems to be devoted to obtaining our earthly wants. And even when we feel it is wrong to seek anxiously these things, we are not willing to give up worrying and give ourselves in complete confidence and trust to God. Think of the many times you worried about a problem. You couldn't think of anything else; it absorbed all your attention. And whether it was solved or not, *time alone usually took care of it.* Meanwhile all that time was wasted. If you are destined to be a worrier then worry about your soul instead of your material needs.

APPLICATION

Cry out your needs to God in prayers but do not cry about them. He knows *the things you need and will give you that which will draw you closest to Him . . . not closer to earth. Look around you this Lent. Listen to those who cry out in need to you and then try your best to fulfill that need.*

First Sunday of Lent, Cycle C #24

READING 2

"Confess With Your Lips That Jesus Is Lord . . ." (Rom. 10: 8-13).

Thought

What we *feel in our heart* is not always easy to *express with our lips.*

Even with those we love on earth, in spite of the great respect and admiration we have for them, we sometimes find it difficult to put our feelings into words. So they really never know how we feel about them. With God it is the same way. Oh, it is true that God *knows* what is in our heart. He does not have to hear any profession of love from our lips . . . *but those around us do.* They have to have some visible sign or proof of our faith, in our speech and in our actions, to motivate them to seek God also. Faith is not just a verbal professing of our belief, not merely giving our consent to the Scriptures, nor simply joining the Church. It is something that we *really feel in our heart* and *all our actions give proof of it.*

Application

Speaking about God, bringing Him into your conversation is not difficult at all. You do not have to quote the Scriptures or give lectures. Just acknowledging some of your blessings in front of your neighbors is a good start . . . e.g. "Thank God for such a beautiful day" . . . "I thank God I have such nice neighbors" . . . "I sure was grateful to God that my son wasn't hurt" etc.

First Sunday of Lent, Cycle C #24

GOSPEL

"Throw Yourself Down from Here . . ." (Lk. 4: 1-13).

Thought

God takes care of us in danger *the way that is best* . . . but it is wrong to presume *we can put Him to the test.*

The devil saw that the temptation of food and riches would not work with Jesus, so he sought to tempt Him to live recklessly; to use faith like a "lucky charm." Jesus plainly showed us we must never expose ourselves rashly to danger in the hope that He will save us. A person willingly getting hooked on drugs, endangering his mind and body, should not presume that God will preserve him from harm and not let him "blow his mind." A man throwing himself off a high cliff or driving down the highway at 100 m.p.h. with the presumption that God will take care of him, no doubt, will be taken care of . . . but mainly by the morgue.

Application

There are times when we have to take prudent risks. We have to do things that might seem reckless, that might even endanger our life . . . saving some one from drowning, from a burning building, etc. But these risks are different. They have some one else in mind . . . not self. Do not make trial of the Lord by doing reckless things, presuming He will protect you from your own foolhardiness. God gave you a mind and a free will. You are expected to use them wisely.

Monday of the 1st Week of Lent #225

READING 1

"You Shall Not Lie or Speak Falsely to One Another . . ."
(Lv. 19: 1-2, 11-18).

Thought

Probably the commonest form of untruthfulness is due to *timidity* . . . mental and moral panic.

We know we *ought to* tell the truth, we *intend to* tell the truth, but under the influence of fear we often *resort to lies as the easiest way out*. We can label it as not wanting to hurt someone's feelings, or not wanting to get a person riled up, or a dozen other things, but it still is lying. We were not brave enough to "tell it like it is." So we add cowardice as well as lying to our makeup. It takes courage to tell the truth, especially when faced with the bare consequences of what might happen when we do. But being realistic and facing the consequences NOW is better than stretching the torment out into the FUTURE. The fear of being found out and the uncertainty of what that will bring can be worse than the punishment itself. Do not let fear of man's punishment make you lie; it is God's punishment you should worry about for not telling the truth.

Application

It is not always easy to tell the truth particularly if you've already suffered before under some one's explosive wrath. At least you know what to expect! And that explosive correction could very well be the tool God is using to keep you in line. Let the unpleasant experience make you more considerate of others when they tell a truth that upsets you or tell you an obvious lie.

Monday of the 1st Week of Lent #225

GOSPEL

"Lord, When Did We See You Hungry . . . ?" (Mt. 25: 31-46).

Thought

There is no charge for crimes of omission in civil law . . . *but there is in Heaven.*

How quickly some of us would ask the same question of Jesus: " 'Lord, when did we see you hungry or thirsty or away from home or naked or ill or in prison and not attend you in your needs?' (v. 44). We gave money to the missions and various drives at church and in the community. They were supposed to dole out the money to cover all those needs. *Yes, Lord, we did all those things!*" It is strange how it never enters our mind that Jesus meant we *personally* were to fill the needs of those around us:

That we are supposed to provide food and drink for the needy family down the street . . . and if we are not well off enough to provide this alone, we can enlist the help of others.

That we are supposed to help find a place for some one to live. We may not have room in our own house but we can help search the area for an empty house.

That we are to provide clothing for those we see in need or know to be in need. We probably have extra clothes hanging in the closet.

That we are supposed to look in on the elderly or the sick to see what we can do for them. Maybe we can take them to the doctor or get food and medicine for them.

That we should have compassion for those in prison, and be kind and helpful to their families outside.

Yes, it never *really struck us* that what we do for the least of our brothers we REALLY DO FOR CHRIST.

Application

A wrong-doer is not always one who has done something; he can also be one who has not done something . . . something that God placed there for him to do. Look for ways to serve God among those around you.

Tuesday of the 1st Week of Lent #226

READING 1

"Achieving the End For Which I Sent It . . ."
(Is. 55: 10-11).

Thought

We cannot always achieve the best conceivable, but we can always *achieve the best possible.*

God gave all of us certain jobs to do and we are responsible for doing them. Yes, we would all like to do big and important things that would make the world "sit up and take notice," but let's face it . . . it is not "in the books" for all of us. We marvel at the dogged determination of some people to see what we consider *a trivial job* through. Nothing sways them. We go so far as to describe them as stubborn fools, working so hard on something that won't amount to a "hill of beans." But *we are the fools.* They have something we do not have; *perseverance.* They are achieving the best possible out of the talents God has given them.

Application

Stick to the job that you are doing. Never mind how insignificant you might think it is. Stick to it until you finish it, and then with the feeling of achieving something for God *start another project.*

Tuesday of the 1st Week of Lent	#226

GOSPEL

"IN YOUR PRAYER DO NOT RATTLE ON LIKE THE PAGANS . . ."
(Mt. 6: 7-15).

THOUGHT

The *tone* of the rattle takes on the *quality of the rattler.*

Nine-day novenas, First Friday devotions, etc. were not given to us as *lucky number combinations.* They are not *magic formulas* to get anything we want from God just by "sheer multiplication" of them. They were given to us for the intention of awakening in us *the need of setting aside some time for* prayer everyday. Some of us *do set aside* some time for prayers everyday, but it is just something we go through as a ritual. And unless we had a set time or placed our book in a certain way, we could not really be sure if we said the prayers or not. We were not really praying. *We were just rattling off some words.* Some parrots can readily repeat over and over again prayers that were taught to them . . . but no one would say they are praying!

APPLICATION

Formal ordinary prayer certainly has its place in our life. But if you notice, in time of need, we find we change our pace. We are suddenly awakened to the fact that our ordinary way of praying . . . just rattling off words . . . is not really adequate. We feel the need of speaking sincerely to God and really telling Him what is in our heart. Try to pray like this all the time . . . listen to the words you are saying in your praying. It should be a time of closeness to God, a time to talk to Him . . . not at Him.

Wednesday of the 1st Week of Lent #227

READING 1

"God Saw By Their Actions . . ." (Jon. 3: 1-10).

Thought

A lot of action does not necessarily *produce progress*.

A hamster on a treadmill certainly shows a lot of action, but who would say he is making any progress or getting any place? Of course, it is impressive to the eye. A lot of us are like that. We have a hundred and one projects going at the same time. We are ever so busy trying to impress others, trying to be "a big wheel." It is a pity that *gaining the attention of others* is much too often the sum and substance of our reason for doing things. And after we have made an impression . . . if we do . . . What then? Back on the treadmill to keep up the pace or no one will be impressed anymore. The only actions that have lasting value are those done for God.

Application

A lot of activity but seldom doing anything well does not make us a "big wheel" in any one's eyes. We do not need to impress God. He sees by our actions how we are but he is more interested in our inner motive. *Concentrate on pleasing God first and it will show in all your actions toward others.* Leave the impression until the final reckoning.

Wednesday of the 1st Week of Lent   #227

GOSPEL

"It Seeks a Sign . . ." (Lk. 11: 29-32).

Thought

Seeking a sign in itself is not an evil, but *needing a visible sign for proof* shows lack of faith.

We often lay down our own certain specifications *for God to follow*. He must do a certain thing at a certain time just to prove He is really up there. When we seek and *demand* a visible sign for proof of faith, it really means we are not totally committed in our belief of God. We are sort of "on the fence" and we can go either way. If the sign comes up to our expectation, we will believe. If not, we will look elsewhere. There is always the possibility that we would be so *taken up with the sign* that we would *overlook the source* from which it came. A man who thinks he has seen something beyond the ordinary, such as a flying saucer, becomes so taken up with talking about it, describing every little detail, that he does not give much thought as to *why* he might have seen it.

Application

God makes allowances for our foolishness; for our silly demands to prove our convictions. There is nothing wrong in asking God for visible things, as long as at the same time you remind him of your willingness to accept however and whenever He decides to carry them out.

Thursday of the 1st Week of Lent #228

READING 1

"Seized With Mortal Anguish ..." (Est. C, 12: 14-16, 23-25).

Thought

"Mortal anguish" is capable of *destroying us* spiritually as well as physically.

Anguish can often impair and imperil our relationship with God. It disturbs our peace of mind and we are inclined to *dwell upon ourselves in self-pity*. There is such a sense of loss and helplessness that we are not sure in which direction to turn. In a moment of weakness we may feel God has forgotten us; He has forsaken us. We feel so alone, so troubled with anguish that at times we cannot even pray. *We panic and shut God out.* It is no wonder we are so fearful and disturbed. Jesus suffered this feeling in the Garden of Gethsemane *to place anguish on a spiritual plane;* to give us a more complete identification with Him. *He knows what we are going through.* He taught us to turn to our Heavenly Father, to pray, to tell him exactly how we feel.

Application

If you think back a week, a month, or a year, or more, of the anguish you felt over various things in your life, you can see it all passed away. You survived it. *The anguish you feel now will also pass away . . . but meanwhile DO NOT WASTE IT. Turn to God. Accept these feelings without complaint as your sacrifice for Lent.*

Thursday of the 1st Week of Lent #228

GOSPEL

"Knock, and It Will Be Opened to You . . ." (Mt. 7: 7-12).

Thought

A person who expects a door "to open" *without his knocking on it* can expect to be *left outside* most of the time.

Even the electric-eye doors, which seem to take all the effort out of getting a door open, *need our co-operation.* We have to stand within a certain area to give indication of our desire to enter. These doors have no doubt spoiled us. Instead of being grateful for such an effortless way of entering, we carry on when we have to shove open the more conventional ones. God surrounds us with a world filled with doors of opportunity. But we have to make our own choices and *do our own knocking* if we want them opened for us. With so many doors it is not always easy to select the right one. But do not worry about that. The main thing is to *get started knocking.* If it is opened and you see it is the wrong one, then close it and start knocking again on the next one.

Application

You may delay doing things but time will not wait for you. Opportunities become fewer as the days go rolling by. *Things may come to those who wait patiently . . .* but they come a lot quicker if you go after them.

Friday of the 1st Week of Lent #229

READING 1

"None of His Virtuous Deeds Shall Be Remembered . . ."
(Ez. 18: 21-28).

Thought

Trying to live the rest of your life *on the merit of past virtuous deeds* is like trying to live a lifetime on past drinks of water. *It needs replenishing.*

The fact that we have begun well is not necessarily a guarantee that we will end well. As we say that *as long as there is life there is hope,* so also we must say *as long as there is life there is danger.* There is never a time in our life when we can let down in our efforts; a time when we think we have done enough to carry us on to Heaven. It is possible for the best years of our life to be swallowed up, marred by pride; — a pride which makes us boastfully point out to others our accomplishments and bask in the sunshine of our past efforts. Or by going to the other extreme . . . wallowing in self-pity, feeling defeated and useless when we can no longer do the things we used to do.

Application

A fresh touch with God at Mass each day provides assurance against this tragedy. Everyday you live God has something for YOU to accomplish, *even if it is just a cheery smile to give someone else encouragement. Seek constantly to serve God through others. Prayers for others in the autumn years of your life* may be the most important assignment God has given you.

Friday of the 1st Week of Lent   #229

GOSPEL

"Recall That Your Brother Has Anything Against You . . ." (Mt. 5: 20-26).

Thought

The forgiving part is *fairly easy,* but not being able to *bring it up* to the person at a later date is *difficult.*

I think we would all agree that to be always forgiving, kind, and helpful is the thing to do. At least we agree in the theory but not always in practice. This type of forgiveness is very familiar . . . "Oh, I forgave him for the dirty deal he gave me. I just don't want to have him around me. That's all!" With all that bitterness we can readily see *there has been no forgiveness at all.* Or we say we forgive some one and then, every chance we get we bring up the topic of our "so-called" forgiveness. Like a sword hanging over some one's head, we threaten to let it fall *if our terms of forgiveness* are not met.

Application

Forgiveness is not a partial thing. You either forgive completely with no strings attached, *never bringing up the subject again,* or you are not really forgiving at all. *And it is not just saying to yourself "I forgive him." It is actually going to the other party and* making sure he knows he is forgiven *and that all ill-will and bitterness are gone.*

Saturday of the 1st Week of Lent #230

READING 1

"You are to Be a People Peculiarly His Own . . ."
(Dt. 26: 16-19).

Thought

A person acting peculiarly usually has a distinguishing mark that *makes him different from others.*

Acting "peculiarly" is not necessarily "an odd ball" doing crazy things; it is one who by his actions, is set aside from the rest of the group. As a people of God, "a people peculiarly his own" (v. 18), *we should be different.* Our love of God *should show* in all our actions to such an extent that non-Christians would automatically know we are Christians. It is said that a man worked for an atheist organization for twenty years. They never discovered or even suspected he was not one of them . . . much less a Catholic! What a waste of years his life must have been. How many of us could easily have worked side by side with him?

Application

There is a difference in just being *a member of the Church and really* feeling *you are one; in the first case you* merely proclaim you are a member by word of mouth, in the other you really prove what you claim to be by your actions. *Which one are you? If you are the first, there is nothing holding you back from being the second one. Become active in your parish work.*

Saturday of the 1st Week of Lent   #230

GOSPEL

"My Command to You Is: Love Your Enemies . . ."
(Mt. 5: 43-48).

Thought

Love our enemies? Yes, even though we have enough trouble *remembering to love our friends* at times.

There are different kinds of love. One has to do with affection and the other with good will. Sympathy, kindness, and appreciation are not just *luxuries reserved for our friends.* They are *obligations* of good will to be shown to *everyone.* Of course, it is easier to do kind things for those who are kind to us. The reward of their pleasure, their gratitude makes us happy. Helping them is easier than helping those who are apt to grumble and find displeasure with us. But Jesus made it clear with his words: "My *command* to you is: love your enemies . . ." (v. 44). So love them we must. The negative attitude of *not harming* our enemies is not sufficient. Nor do we fulfill our Christian duty by *avoiding* them. We do not have to seek them out . . . round them up . . . to force our love on them. But if we encounter them in our normal pattern of living, we are not to be antagonistic or rude. We are to be charitable and treat them in the same manner as we do our friends.

Application

Jesus, by his example, showed us that love always wins in the end. *It may work ever so slowly and there may not be much evidence at first . . . but it works. It will conquer hatred. Hatred can only thrive with two parties being at odds. Make sure you are not at odds with anyone.*

2nd Sunday of Lent, Cycle A — #25

READING 1

"I Will Make Your Name Great So That You Will Be a Blessing . . ." (Gn. 12: 1-4).

Thought

Some are not satisfied with God making the greatness; they prefer *to make their own greatness.*

Some men labor for a lifetime devising all forms of strategy and human ingenuity in an attempt to make their name immortal. They want to leave behind them a magnificent granite monument with their name etched in it. They want all the world to know . . . *they were here.* They cannot endure the thought of being forgotten. God does not disparage the idea of "doing" in relation to salvation. We are expected to do our best. But when we *exclude God* and go about trying to make a name for ourselves, trying so hard to be important that our sole aim is *material gain and fame,* then that acquired name will be strictly of earthly value. And what good is a granite monument on earth if we have *a monument of blazing hot coals* when we leave this earth?

Application

In this life we are given to exaggerating *the worth of things around us . . . and more so our own worth. But the time will come when our values will be revised by God, when we will see things as they are. Don't worry about a name. Do your work for God. Let Him make your name great.*

2nd Sunday of Lent, Cycle A   #25

READING 2

"BEAR YOUR SHARE OF THE HARDSHIP . . ." (2 Tm. 1: 8-10).

THOUGHT

Bearing your share *with God* may not remove the hardship, but it gives a *divine purpose to it.*

We do not mind getting our share of all the good things in life, but anything that even looks like a hardship makes us wince. We would just as soon let some one else have that share. *We already did.* We let Jesus have *most* of it when He suffered and died on the cross for us. The word "share" gives us comfort, for it means that *we are not alone;* some one is sharing with us. But *your share* belongs *exclusively to you.* No one else can bear it for you. There are many hardships and tragedies which break our heart and seem almost too much to bear. But we do bear them . . . once we decide to pick them up and *share them with God.*

APPLICATION

Standing outside, looking at your share of something to be done can discourage you. Of course, looking at it from the inside may do the same thing, but at least you can be encouraged by the fact that you had enough gumption to start. You can easily handle one day's burden but do not add yesterday's and tomorrow's. *You are bound to be crushed. Concentrate on today's.* You have what it takes to get you through. You have God!

2nd Sunday of Lent, Cycle A   #25

GOSPEL

"With Your Permission I Will Erect Three Booths . . ."
(Mt. 17: 1-9).

Thought

We sometimes speak from our *feelings* rather than from our *intelligence*.

Many times, like Peter, we are "taken back" . . . surprised by some unforeseen event that happens. We want to *do something* to show what we feel. We do not know what to do. So we just open our mouth and speak. And invariably our impulsive words are apt to be on the *impractical side*. We talk about doing things that will sidetrack our energy and *do no one any good*. We know it as soon as we have spoken, but to *save face*, we may feel we have to carry it through. Think long and seriously before embarking on a scheme that may cost you and others time and money.

Application

If you have "bitten off more than you can chew" with your too hasty, impulsive words . . . be humble enough to admit you were wrong. A moment's embarrassment may save you a lifetime of regret.

2nd Sunday of Lent, Cycle B

READING 1

"God Put Abraham to the Test . . ." (Gn. 22: 1-2, 9, 10-13 15-18).

Thought

We wouldn't mind being *put to the test* if the *results always turned out like Abraham's.*

In school we learned that the purpose of a test was to give *proof* of what we had learned. And when we failed in the test, it proved we needed more study, more help in that subject. We can apply the same reasoning to our faith. We feel pretty sure, pretty secure with the *little knowledge* we have. But when we are "put to the test" by God, we find our knowledge is not adequate. We fail! We fail because we did not really know much at all about the subject of faith or about God. Continue to learn, to grow in your faith. If bad eye-sight keeps you from reading, you can always listen more closely to the sermons the priest gives. Take a thought home with you from Mass. You might have passed all the tests before with "flying colors" but do you have enough knowledge to pass all those that may come in the future?

Application

The testing of your faith can be expected. But from our own experiences in life, we know that all tests do not end so happily as Abraham's did. . . . So be prepared for some rough times. No do we really give up all attachment to the things we offer as sacrifice as Abraham did. *We want to feel,* and do feel *big and important with the offering we make as a sacrifice, but often it i only a half-hearted offering. In the back of our mind* we hope tha God will not take all of it. *Prove your worth by giving whole heartedly, without reneging and without complaint.*

2nd Sunday of Lent, Cycle B #26

READING 2

"IF GOD IS FOR US, WHO CAN BE AGAINST US?"
(Rom. 8: 31-34).

THOUGHT

You can always *depend upon God* being on your side, but can God *depend upon you* being on His side?

St. Paul points out to us that no enemy of man can destroy our relationship with God. Distress, misfortune, temptation, fame, death, etc. — none of these things can harm or lessen the security we have in God's love. None of it can touch our soul . . . *unless we let it do so.* Whatever happens to us is working towards God's design. *He knows what He is doing.* He is on our side; *He is for us.* But His just being on our side is not enough. We have to co-operate freely and whole-heartedly so that He can carry out His purpose. *We have to be on His side also.*

APPLICATION

Do not fear to tackle anything. If you think you are in a situation that seems beyond your ability, why worry? When God has work to do, He either finds or makes an instrument *fit to carry it out. He will make you a fit instrument too, if you submit your will and co-operate with Him. He is on your side . . . if you let Him be. Plunge right in and do whatever is before you.*

2nd Sunday of Lent, Cycle B #26

GOSPEL

"He Was Transfigured Before Their Eyes . . ."
(Mk. 9: 2-10).

Thought

A school boy's description of the transfiguration: The day the Lord got "lit up."

We can get "lit up" also. Similar to a light switch, we can accept grace or reject grace. We can turn it "off and on" by our own free will. We know that sometimes when we try the switch, nothing happens; the bulb is burned out. That is what happens when mortal sin enters our life. The sin destroys the main element . . . grace. We can see a little but our vision has been impaired. We stumble around in the darkness seeking to find our way. *But we need more light!* And like a small boy, who needs help from his father to change the bulb high up in the ceiling, we have to go to our Father and tell Him what has happened . . . CONFESSION . . . and He quickly sets things right again.

Application

God sets things right again for us in confession, but the wattage of the light that shines in us depends upon the effort we want to put forth. *Go to confession and be determined to do better than you have ever done before.* You are bound to succeed if you have that determination. *Faith helps us only in the proportion to the effort we put into it.*

2nd Sunday of Lent, Cycle C #27

READING 1

"A Deep, Terrifying Darkness Enveloped Him . . ." (Gn. 15: 5-12, 17-18).

Thought

Darkness may be needed to bring out the stars, but most of us would *prefer to have the sun shine all the time.*

We do not usually think of a terrifying darkness in our life as a sign of our Lord making a covenant with us: doing something that will be a blessing for us. We are more apt to think of it as a *punishment.* But just as a developer of photos has to work in a dark place to get a clear image on his picture, so it is that *darkness is needed in our life to get a clearer image of God.* The bright lights of *the world of "everything going right"* has a way of distorting our image of God. The picture of "self" overshadows the view of God. Darkness challenges energy and perseverance in us. It calls into activity the strongest qualities of our faith. We are made to search the inmost corner of our soul for lights we have not been called upon to use before. In the house we usually have candles or a lamp stored away for emergencies when the electricity goes off. We have all had to use them at one time or another. In the night of trouble, we also have *some lamps to be enkindled within us.* We might have to search for them if it has been a long time since they've been used, but *you will find the light* if you search hard enough.

Application

We are all haunted and terrified at times by the darkness of fear, frustration, and failure. And they terrify us mostly because they are beyond our control; *we cannot see a way out. Yet, we know that God is* always in control *of all situations. Is it that we do not have enough faith in Him? Regardless of the most discouraging circumstances JUST HANG ON TO GOD. He will see you through.*

2nd Sunday of Lent, Cycle C #27

READING 2

"THEIR GOD IS THEIR BELLY . . ." (Phil. 3: 17, 4: 1).

THOUGHT

There are always a lot of *defenders* of over-indulgence but they offer *no real defense for it.*

Food and drink were meant for our nourishment, not for our *destruction!* We should eat and drink to live, not live to eat and drink. When a person ruins his health for the sake of the pleasures of the table or the bottle . . . he is abusing God's gifts. All of us know somebody who, despite a doctor's warning about restricting food and drink, says: "Eating and drinking is all I have in life. I'm going to do what I please!" If this is all he has in life, his life is pitifully empty. And in his last agonizing years of ill-health, the "pleasing of the senses" *that brought on his condition* will give him little comfort. Temperance in managing your senses is more than controlled emotion. It is also a habit of *controlled judgment . . . self-discipline.* When your children and those around you see discipline of your senses in you . . . or the lack of discipline . . . the natural inclination is to duplicate the pattern within themselves. Parents cannot train their children to go in one direction and except them to turn out well *if they go in the opposite direction.*

APPLICATION

It is never too late to change or moderate your pattern of eating, drinking, or smoking. Lent is a good time to start. Just try doing without a little bit less each day. *You cannot do it alone or you would have done so before.* Earnestly ask God to help you. *MAKE SOME EFFORT. Even if you cut down a little bit, it will be an improvement!*

2nd Sunday of Lent, Cycle C #27

GOSPEL

"And Went Up Onto a Mountain to Pray . . ." (Lk. 9: 28-36).

Thought

Going up onto a mountain to pray is *exhilarating*, but few men want to *stay there*.

There is something we feel when we stand high up on a mountain, looking out over the world below. It is an awesome, almost holy type of feeling and we are somewhat reluctant to leave. Yet, we would get fearful if we thought we were going to be *stuck up there*. Peter also wanted to stay there on the mountain top and even build three booths. Yet he became fearful when God spoke from the cloud. His enthusiasm was replaced by fear and awe at the unveiled glory of God. *His unworthiness silenced his lips.* We have great aspirations and like to contemplate holiness. We even strive a little towards it, but we are a little afraid of really attaining it. The awareness of our own unworthiness makes us want to give up before we start.

Application

Jesus became transfigured to show us that we will be transfigured too, if we follow Him. *Don't worry about your unworthiness. At least a person who feels low with unworthiness may see a glimpse of Heaven once in awhile* when he looks up to God. But the person who thinks he is so high up in the world that he can only look down on others *is apt to see another place more clearly! Strive towards holiness by preparing yourself step by step.* Go to Mass, read spiritual books, live your faith. Each step draws you closer to your goal . . . God.

Monday of the 2nd Week of Lent   #231

READING 1

"Justice, O Lord, Is on Your Side . . ." (Dn. 9: 4-10).

Thought

We always welcome justice *unless* we feel it is doing an *injustice to us.*

We are apt to think of justice as something that goes on or is settled only in a courtroom. We prefer to have it *more on our side* to assure us of getting what we want. But justice is impartial. It treats *all alike* and not according to the degree of how much we like or dislike somebody. None of us can escape it. If we rebel against the laws of God or the laws of the land we automatically throw ourselves under the wheels of justice. The wheels of justice do not discriminate; they crush whatever is in its path. Oh, we may *seem to escape* the punishment for a while, but at the Last Judgment it will be brought before us. Justice *is* on God's side but so is His mercy. If we stay on His side it will never hurt us.

Application

According to St. Thomas: "Justice is the firm and constant will to give to each one his due." But justice takes on a different look when we think of it as being free to do right things because we LIKE TO DO RIGHT, *rather than* doing right because we will be punished if we do wrong. *Justice comes from the heart and influences all we do. It is a quality that deals with all forms of what we call fairness: honesty, truthfulness, charity, keeping promises, etc.*

Monday of the 2nd Week of Lent #231

GOSPEL

"For the Measure You Measure With Will Be Measured Back to You" (Lk. 6: 36-38).

Thought

Unless the *measuring is accurate,* in spite of the most expensive ingredients used, *nothing will come out as it was designed.* It is bound to be inferior and collapse.

There are many kinds of measurements, as well as ways of using them, to accomplish what should be done. Some of us make our measures full and overflowing, some with great exactness, some with a scant measure, and some hardly get the bottom of the cup covered. Whatever measure we use in our acts of charity, large or small, God tells us that is the measure He will use to give back to us. There is a difference between *knowing the right scale of values for doing things* and *having the right sense of values when doing them.* Unless we have the *right spirit* . . . LOVE . . . our acts of charity are just burdensome things we do to get them over; they are not really things done to please God at all.

Application

Some of us love to do all the measuring, finding out exactly what should be used, how it should be done, but we never get down to the nitty gritty part of doing it. *Our measures for God through others are to be distributed NOW and not put off until we have finished* taking our own portions. *Do it now. Too soon it will be too late. And there may be no time left for compassion; no time left to feed the hungry; no time left to comfort the troubled soul; no time left for generous impulses.*

Tuesday of the 2nd Week of Lent #232

READING 1

"COME NOW, LET US SET THINGS RIGHT . . ." (Is. 1: 10, 16-20).

THOUGHT

Before you can "set things right" you have to *see that they are wrong.*

There can be *no delusion with God* but there can be *plenty of delusion with yourself.* Unless you honestly look into your own heart, lay your life right out before God exactly like it is, and *want to change what you see there,* you can not even start to "set things right." What you see may frighten you. But you need not get frustrated or feel hopeless. The text says, "Let US set things right" (v. 18). "Us" means . . . not you alone . . . but *God and you. You together* can set things right. So relax, God already knows all about you and He still loves you. He wants you to know all about yourself so you can really work on loving Him. But seeing is not enough. You can not expect God to *take away your sins* until you are ready to *acknowledge them and let go of them.* "Though your sins be like scarlet, they may become white as snow . . ." (v. 18).

APPLICATION

The important thing to remember is that you are never a hopeless case. *When you fail, when you stray away for a short time . . . or even a long time . . .* you can always come back. *Let God help you set things right in the sacrament of penance.*

Tuesday of the 2nd Week of Lent #232

GOSPEL

"Do Everything and Observe Everything They Tell You. But Do Not Follow Their Example" (Mt. 23: 1-12).

Thought

We have to learn to distinguish between some one's *teaching* and his *practice.*

We can be so *impressed* by the pious words of somebody, that under that *influence* we may be fooled into believing it is all right *to follow his example also.* We may think that anything he does *must be all right.* Or on the other hand, when we see that a person's actions are so obviously *contrary* to the words he is using to instruct us, we lose all faith in him and are apt *to discard all he is telling us.* We may think that way about our priests sometimes. But we are wrong. *God uses all kinds of instruments* to teach us the truths necessary to draw us closer to him. Never mind about how those in authority act; their conduct has nothing to do with our being obedient to the laws of God. The weaknesses, the faults, the dispositions of a priest are no greater nor less than any man's . . . except that he *should be trying to control them better* because of his high calling.

Application

Every Christian, however advanced in spiritual life he thinks he is, must respect the Church and its authority; he must do as it bids him to do. The devil likes to use our own personal likes and dislikes as a tool to influence us . . . to keep us from Mass. It is such a natural feeling that we may get involved deeply before we realize it is pulling us from God. Put aside your feelings. You go to Mass to worship God . . . not the priests! Pray for those in authority.

Wednesday of the 2nd Week of Lent #233

READING 1

"Let Us Carefully Note His Every Word . . ."
(Jer. 18: 18-20).

Thought

Noting every word to gain knowledge *to better yourself* is good; to gain knowledge *to ruin somebody* is not.

These men listened carefully to every word the Prophet said, not to learn from him, but in the hope of finding something to turn against him. We are also like that at times. If we cannot get somebody to do what we want, we may resort to lies to harm him. Lying in itself is an evil but when we misrepresent the facts and twist the words of truth to use them against a person, we add injury to the lying. And the worst part is *we never distort by ourselves*. We want company so it always involves somebody else. Consoling ourselves that we aren't telling any lies . . . we are only repeating the truth . . . does not take away from our *malicious intent*.

Application

Whenever we indulge in deceit we damage our own character as well as the innocent victim. We undermine our self-respect, become hypocritical, and poison our outlook on life. Not to mention how much it weakens our faith. Work on this during Lent. Pray for those you might have harmed. Ask God for the strength and wisdom not to be deceitful again. Try to right the wrong the best you can.

Wednesday of the 2nd Week of Lent #233

GOSPEL

"The Other Ten, on Hearing This, Became Indignant At the Two Brothers . . ." (Mt. 20: 17-28).

Thought

We have no right to become "indignant" because somebody else asks for a favor that we were *not brave enough to ask for ourselves.*

Silence can be a sign of strength, but it can also be a sign of *cowardice.* Indignation should express *disapproval* of some one's dishonorable or unworthy action . . . not *jealousy and envy* because we did not do something ourselves. Usually the person we are upset about has done nothing wrong. Nor has he in anyway transgressed any of our rights. We are just upset because we lacked the courage and did not dare to speak up for ourselves. Pride has a sneaky way of entering in dozens of innocent ways to accomplish what the devil wants it to do.

Application

There are times when we should be bold. *It is always better to* ask *and* have a refusal *than to hesitate timidly, and find out after the opportunity has passed, that* you would not have been refused. *Do not let your pride . . . the embarrassment of perhaps being refused . . . hold you back.*

Thursday of the 2nd Week of Lent   #234

READING 1

"TO REWARD EVERYONE ACCORDING TO HIS WAYS . . ."
(Jer. 17: 5-10).

THOUGHT

A "reward" is really *getting exactly what you deserve.*

The object of a reward is to give something in return for an action performed. The action could be good or it could be bad. Much too often we associate a reward with only an *achievement of something good;* like a merit of award or a medal of distinction. But it could very well be *a reward of punishment* if it is what we deserve for the action we have done. If we were as aware of the reward for the evil we do, as much as we are for the good, it might make us stop and think a little before we act.

APPLICATION

"To reward everyone according to his ways" (v. 10) . . . is quite a sobering thought . . . especially if our ways have not been too good. *It is never too late to change. Start anew. Change your ways and do a little more than required to try to make up for the past. Lent is a good time to start.*

Thursday of the 2nd Week of Lent   #234

GOSPEL

"At His Gate Lay a Beggar . . ." (Lk. 16: 10-31).

Thought

We learn to *love people through God,* but it is more important to *love God through people.*

Many may think quite highly of themselves that they are fulfilling the law of God . . . of loving their neighbors . . . simply because they do not hate them. They have a neutral or indifferent attitude; they live their lives and the neighbors live theirs. But the fact that they *never feel any responsibility* for causing or relieving their neighbor's sorrowful plight does not excuse them. It shows they do not love them. It is a sin of omission against Christian charity. If we are true followers of Christ, we will turn from our small world of narrow selfishness, and with true concern seek out those in need.

Application

We turn away with scorn sometimes from a person who is in need and begs from us. We excuse ourselves from the obligation of charity with "Let him get a job and earn his own money!" It is not for us to judge *the beggar. It is for us to give alms cheerfully. St. Francis taught us that no one in need should ever be turned away.*

Friday of the 2nd Week of Lent #235

READING 1

"They Hated Him So Much That They Would Not Even Greet Him . . ." (Gn. 37: 3-4, 12-13, 17-28).

Thought

Hatred and revenge might *satisfy our pride* but it does not *satisfy our conscience.*

Joseph's brothers coveted the special favors shown by their father. It turned them into envious and jealous men who were discontented and dissatisfied with what they themselves possessed. Hatred often makes us victims of a bitter and intense struggle *that sours and destroys our own character.* It narrows and discolors our thinking, biases all our judgments, and does a thorough job of corrupting our conscience. Foolish spite makes us sullen and morose. We do not speak to some people for years. Miserable misunderstandings carry on so long that we forget what even started them. We keep hate-filled quarrels alive because *we cannot sacrifice our pride* and put an end to them.

Application

Hatred, like a worm in an apple, makes such a small hole when it enters, but it is capable of destroying the whole inside if left in there long enough. *Face and discuss your hatred with someone you trust and you will soon be rid of it. Make a determined effort this Lent to mend the hurt feelings of the past.*

Friday of the 2nd Week of Lent #235

GOSPEL

"Although They Sought to Arrest Him They Had Reason to Fear the Crowds . . ." (Mt. 21: 33-43, 45-46).

Thought

At times *fear* of something seems to have a better hold on our actions than *love*.

There are many things we *might* do if fear did not hold us back. Fear, although it is not the best motive, is a *necessary ingredient* in our life that helps *to keep us in line*. It makes us think twice before engaging in something that might bring any *retaliation*. Of course, it is really our own self-preservation we are thinking about! For some people *fear of man* seems topmost in their thoughts. *Fear of God seldom seems to enter the picture.*

Application

Pay heed to the feeling of fear and apprehension which holds you back from doing something that is questionable. Consider it as a warning from God *and think twice before acting. It may be the means of saving you . . . soul-wise . . . from self-destruction!*

READING 1

"But Delights Rather in Clemency . . ."
(Mi. 7: 14-15, 18-20).

Thought

When we *receive* clemency it is a delight. When we are *dispensing* it . . . *is it a delight?*

Spontaneous love and clemency are *the marks of a Christian*. We all know what it is like to feel heavy with guilt and remorse; the object of *deserved* condemnation. Then the person we have wronged comes along. With great clemency he forgives us readily . . . and cheerfully. The weight is suddenly lifted. It fills us so full of joy and relief that we feel like a new person. We are determined to do better from that moment on. We are delighted with clemency. But when the shoe is on the other foot, the delight does not come so easy. The other party has offended us; he *deserves* to be condemned. To deal with him with clemency . . . and find delight in that . . . there is the rub! Yet, this is what the Reading today wants us to do: to take delight in showing mercy to somebody who does not deserve it.

Application

A person who speaks and acts unkindly already feels **unkindly**. *He needs to be calmed, not aroused and provoked into* more *unkindness. Perhaps he is not feeling well, the whole day went wrong; he is just in a bad mood. Have compassion. Speak calmly and gently* or do not speak at all. *Delight in clemency.*

Saturday of the 2nd Week of Lent #236

GOSPEL

"Give Me the Share of the Estate That Is Coming to Me . . ." (Lk. 15: 1-3, 11-32).

Thought

The demand of "give me" should also be accompanied by the *acceptance* of "getting what's coming to you" *after you've used up* what you've been given.

There is something of the prodigal son as well as the older son in all of us. We have moments when we *demand and want* "all that is coming to us." We are not bothered about *what it will cost us in better things* . . . not bothered, that is, *until it starts costing us.* Then we realize our folly. And like the elder son, even when we have "all that is coming to us" and nothing is taken away, we become uncharitable; we get upset about compassion bestowed on another whom we feel is not deserving of it. What fools we are! *Rejoicing in the return of a sinner in no way takes away from our inheritance.* And it certainly will *add* to our spiritual treasury if we rejoice over his conversion.

Application

The main point of the parable is that the younger son came to his senses after his foolishness . . . as we should do after our foolishness. His experience made him a humble person. He acknowledged what he had become with no alibis and no pleading of mitigating circumstances. He gambled everything on his belief that his father would be merciful. And his father was merciful, just as God, our Father, always is. Turn to God. He stands there waiting for your return. Ask Him for mercy.

3rd Sunday of Lent, Cycle A #28

READING 1

"Is the Lord in Our Midst Or Not? . . ." (Ex. 17: 3-7).

Thought

Believing is free but it will cost you to prove that belief.

The people of Israel were willing to follow the Lord *as long as everything was going all right*. But as soon as things got tough, they started grumbling and quarreling with Moses, blaming him for their plight. They forgot all about the Promised Land. *It was lost in the situation at hand*. They wanted *proof* that God was still there. He is always there, but we have come to think that the Lord is only in the midst of good times; times when things are going our way and we have no complaint. We really have no reason to think that. We know that the life of Jesus on earth was certainly not an easy one. He thrived and existed in hardship most of His life. "Is the Lord in our midst or not" (v. 7)? Yes, He is there all right, but we have to open our hearts to acknowledge Him. It is something like a man knocking on the door waiting to be left inside. He is there all right, but *he cannot come inside until we open the door.*

Application

Your faith is not a vague, cold impersonal ideal. It is a living reality that turns your duty into a privilege, your yearning into fulfillment, and all your hardships into achievements. Never mind if things may seem to be all going wrong. God knows it as well as you do. *Trust in Him; He will right them at the best time.*

3rd Sunday of Lent, Cycle A #28

READING 2

"Now That We Have Been Justified By Faith . . ."
(Rom. 5: 1-2, 5-8).

Thought

Being "justified by faith" does not mean we do not have to do anything *to justify our faith.*

"We *have been* justified by faith" (v. 1); Jesus has already fulfilled all the requirements to get us to Heaven. We can be at peace with Him and the world. We do not have to worry and concern ourselves with trying to do big important things beyond our capabilities to save our soul. Just living for and through God is enough. But just *marking time* in your faith and *adding nothing to it* will not assure you a place in Heaven. It is more than *just getting by;* we have to do the ordinary things but do them in *an extraordinary way.*

Application

Some of us think we are a success *at being a Christian just by being MEDIOCRE . . . just barely getting by in our Christian duty. We avoid any concerted effort or "putting ourselves out" for anybody.* Just think of what a success you could be by putting in some extra effort! *Seek ways to help others through acts of kindness that come up in your everyday living. Help some one carry packages, bake a cake for the family of your neighbor who is sick, take an elderly person shopping, etc.*

3rd Sunday of Lent, Cycle A #28

GOSPEL

"BELIEVED IN HIM ON THE STRENGTH OF THE WOMAN'S WORD OF TESTIMONY . . ." (Jn. 4: 5-42).

THOUGHT

Blabbing everything you know is generally not good, but if it is about God, it is perfectly all right. Of course, for some of us *it might not take too long to tell all we know.*

One woman had found her Savior and she could not keep it to herself. *She wanted to tell everyone about Him.* She wanted to share her new found faith. When a great joy comes into our life, it brings with it a feeling of good will and generosity to all. It is like an inner fire that glows warm and bright influencing the whole atmosphere around us. It changes our whole outlook. It kindles the air with hope and encouragement.

APPLICATION

We can be a bottleneck or a channel through which the Word of God is spread. Faith that is real is contagious. *If you* really *love God you will be like the Samaritan woman; you will not be able to keep Him to yourself. You will want to tell all you meet about* **Him.**

3rd Sunday of Lent, Cycle B #29

READING 1

"God Delivered All These Commandments . . ." (Ex. 20: 1-17).

Thought

"Delivering something" does not assure that the recipient is always going *to accept that which is delivered.*

We seem to have lost what some call the "old-fashioned" *directness.* A directness that taught *that breaking God's laws means punishment now and hereafter.* We have substituted a wishy-washy, flabby toleration and *labeled it love.* It *expects* obedience to be achieved from a selfish negative love . . . one that allows everybody to have his own way . . . to do his own thing. Of course, we can see that is a lot of nonsense. The condition of the world today proves that this is not the answer. The commandments will never be "old-fashioned." They are as up-to-date now as when God spoke them. But He did not intend for us to use them as something to enforce, or *hold over somebody's head* as if we were judges and dictators. They were not meant to bind us but *to set us free* in ways of righteousness. They are not contrary at all to our nature; they are divine sanctions of the natural laws already written in our heart.

Application

Loving God with all your heart also includes a reverential fear of offending and losing Him. *Obedience to the Ten Commandments is a sacred obligation for all of us. And unless respect for them is evident in our pattern of living, we cannot expect others who look to us to observe them. Review them often with your family.*

3rd Sunday of Lent, Cycle B #29

READING 2

"God's Folly Is Wiser Than Men, and His Weakness More Powerful Than Men . . ." (1 Cor. 1: 22-25).

Thought

What may seem like a "folly" to one person may be *a wise decision* to another.

Mockers of religious practices or beliefs often "poke fun" at that which they do not have *the wisdom or the courage to embrace themselves.* There are those now, as in St. Paul's day, who pride themselves in their so-called great wisdom to analyze and define religion as "downright foolishness." They think the idea of an omnipotent God inviting mere man to come to Him is certainly confessing a weakness. And it is plain nonsense to believe in that kind of God. But "God's folly is wiser than men, and his weakness more powerful than men" (v. 25). In His wisdom He knew that an action done fully with love . . . *because a person really wants to do something* . . . is certainly more beneficial than one done because of fear of punishment.

Application

St. Francis was often a victim of such mockery and his actions were considered a folly at times. But he never minded that. He was not so much concerned what his action looked like on the outside as he was concerned what it really was in his heart; his motive for doing something. Do not worry what others think about you practicing your religion. Every bit of ridicule suffered in silence will be repaid many times over in grace.

3rd Sunday of Lent, Cycle B   #29

GOSPEL

"Get Them Out of Here! . . ." (Jn. 2: 13-25).

Thought

An outburst of our anger is seldom zeal; it is usually *lack of control* because we did not get our way.

There are times when anger is justified and is the *only means* that will help obtain the results needed. All of your other calm, peaceful ways have failed to help the person. So you give him a blast that draws him up short. *But justified anger ends right there.* It does not hang on, harboring grudges, showing spite or revenge. And always uppermost in your mind should be the welfare of that person. You want him to be *a better person* because of your words of fire . . . not *a bitter person* because of your ire.

Application

No one enjoys being around another, who on the slightest provocation . . . or none at all . . . is liable to flare up and shower one with angry words. If you tend to be quick tempered, try to hold back your words by saying an Our Father before speaking. In the event of failing a few times, say the prayer after your outburst *and after you have said I AM SORRY.*

3rd Sunday of Lent, Cycle C #30

READING 1

"For the Place Where You Stand Is Holy Ground . . ."
(Ex. 3: 1-8, 13-15).

Thought

If we have no reverence and respect for God in his holy place . . . *inside church* . . . we certainly will not have it when *outside the church.*

Much too often nowadays, we forget or overlook the holiness of the place where we stand . . . here in church. Some do not give it anymore thought (or perhaps as much thought) than if they were going on a picnic or a visit to a friend's house. The church is more than just a gathering place for worship. It is a consecrated place: consecrated by the real presence of Christ, the God-Man, in the tabernacle. Moses was told to take off his shoes in reverence; a custom that still exists in certain religions. We are not asked to take off our shoes, but we are asked to dress and act in a manner befitting the holy place where we have come to worship.

Application

The Church does not set itself up as a critic of the fashion designer or styles . . . but you are. And you are expected to use your Christ-like judgment on what to wear to church. What you wear *on the outside* does reflect *what you are on the* inside. How you act *outwardly towards God and your worship also reflects what you are on the inside.* And what you are . . . usually . . . so your children will be.

3rd Sunday of Lent, Cycle C #30

READING 2

"The Things That Happened to Them Serve As an Example . . ." (1 Cor. 10: 1-6, 10-12).

Thought

An example will not help the person who does not realize the example *is for his benefit.*

We seldom see the meaning of the things that are happening to us *at the time they are happening.* We are too wrapped up in the event itself to notice any purpose in it . . . especially if it is something disagreeable. But bringing to mind the past, and the examples and experiences of others, will help us to see more clearly that Divine Providence has a hand in them. The evil and the good events all have a purpose. But some of us do not learn from the experience of others . . . or even from our own. What has happened to another does not serve as an example for us. *We have to learn the hard way;* by our own mistakes. And many times instead of "practice making perfect" for improvement, *it looks like we practice our own mistakes and make them more perfect!*

Application

You should be awake to what goes on: both in yourself and in others. But just observing what is right *in others and* not doing right *yourself won't benefit you.* There is a message there for you. *God is using the example of experience to draw you closer to Himself: by the pleasant things through* gratitude; *by the unpleasant things through* resignation to His holy will.

61

3rd Sunday of Lent, Cycle C   #30

GOSPEL

"Do You Think They Were More Guilty Than Anyone Else . . . ?" (Lk. 13: 1-9).

Thought

One's guilt should be judged by what he has done *not by what is done to him.*

If we measured a man's guilt by the amount of troubles which befall him, Jesus would certainly have been classified as *the champion sinner of all mankind.* Certainly no one had more suffering than He did. Does tragedy come only because of guilt? Our Lord said: "Certainly not! But I tell you, you will all come to the same end unless you begin to reform" (v. 3). He did not "rule out" that tragedy *could be caused by a person's wrong doing.* Many times it does happen because of sin. And when it does, it is God's merciful way of punishing us on earth to enable us to see the folly of our sinful ways before it is too late.

Application

There is the danger of a noxious self-complacency which can accompany the popular thought that misfortune is always the result of sinful actions. *If we have no misfortune in our life we are apt to feel we are doing all right . . . or either getting by with things. Good fortune, ease, and comfort may walk hand in hand with pride, greed, and selfishness. Beware! The boom could lower on you any day. Have compassion. Pray for those who are suffering misfortune. Try to help them in any way you can.*

Optional Mass,* the 3rd Week of Lent #237

READING 1

"Give Us Water to Drink . . ." (Ex. 17: 1-7).

Thought

We might not carry on about any big things, but *the little things can sure get to us.*

We usually think of only *big things* as the cause of quarrels and evil actions, but it is mostly the *common little things* that cause the biggest problems. The sneaky little things that really do not amount to "a hill of beans" . . . a harsh word, a fancied insult, a misconstrued motive, a distorted comment, petty jealousy . . . all small things in themselves, but they can get us into a grouchy, spiteful mood that ruins our disposition and outlook on life. People who are normally good have been known to kill over petty jealousy, a hastily spoken word, and even a drink of water or a bite of food when stranded in the desert. Whereas they might never have killed because of a personal injury, robbery, or even murder of somebody they love.

Application

The devil does not bother about the big problems that crop up. He knows that you are on guard against them and will turn them over to God for help. He concentrates on the unsuspecting little everyday annoyances that you are so sure you can handle. And he makes sure that they get all out of proportion before you are aware of them. Develop a habit of offering everything *to God, and then be patient and charitable while suffering through them.*

---

*This Mass may be used on any day of this week, especially in years B and C when the gospel of the Samaritan woman is not read on the Third Sunday of Lent.

Optional Mass,* the 3rd Week of Lent   #237

GOSPEL

"He Told Me Everything I Ever Did . . ." (Jn. 4: 5-42).

Thought

We feel more at ease with somebody who *really knows what we are.*

The Samaritan woman seemed quite content and exuberant over Jesus knowing all about her; that there was nothing in her life hidden from Him. It is like that also with us when we *really have faith.* We are relieved when we begin to realize that there is Somebody at last *who knows exactly what we are.* There is nothing hidden from Him. The all-seeing, all-knowing God looks into our heart, loves, understands our weaknesses, and is pleased with our most secret thoughts. That is, it is a relief *if our inmost thoughts are worthy of such scrutiny.* Otherwise, it is a little bit *uncomfortable.*

Application

During this Lent, really look into your heart. It is time to give up that pretense and really start correcting *that which needs correcting. Be at ease, not fretful. Your every effort to purge out what you would not want anyone to know will be pleasing to God. Start with a good confession.*

---

*This Mass may be used on any day of this week, especially in years B and C when the gospel of the Samaritan woman is not read on the Third Sunday of Lent.

Monday of the 3rd Week of Lent   #238

READING 1

"If the Prophet Had Told You to Do Extraordinary . . ." (2 Kgs. 5: 1-15).

Thought

If we wait around to do only "extraordinary" things for God, we are liable *to do nothing at all.*

Too many times the value we place on something depends upon how big it is, how hard it is to do, and how astonishing it is. *What it accomplishes seems to be secondary.* Extraordinary things always impress us. They make us feel that *we are really doing something.* It is more of a feeling of *pride* than anything else. If our Lord came down to earth again and handed out a list of extraordinary things to do . . . we would all be standing in line. We would be anxious to receive our assignment. Not that we would carry it out any better than we do now . . . but the novelty of it would attract our attention.

Application

God mostly places ordinary things in our lives. These are the means He wants us to use to draw us closer to Him. If we underestimate or cannot do these common everyday things well, we have no business expecting that we will be able to do any extraordinary thing well . . . if at all.

Monday of the 3rd Week of Lent #238

GOSPEL

"Was Filled With Indignation . . ." (Lk. 4: 24-30).

Thought

Actions do speak louder than words, in fact, so loud that they often *drown out our conscience.*

When we are filled with indignation we burn inside with a mood that cries out for *immediate action.* It distorts our perspective so that what was said or done to us gets out of proportion. We flare up and lose control. We act impulsively, doing things we would normally never do. And sometimes, even when we know the complaint leveled against us was *justified,* because of our hurt pride we still feel indignation. We sound off with a retort in defense of ourselves and make matters even worse. We add fuel to the fire with lies and accusations and *burn the bridge of return* over which we could easily have come back with *an apology* for our action.

Application

Restrain the desire to "get even" with the one who has caused indignation in you. Try to see both sides of the situation. Wait until you have calmed down and reviewed what has happened and then see if any helpful, corrective measures should be taken. If you cannot find anything helpful, then try to put it out of your mind. Pray for the person and be charitable to him. He probably wants to forget his impulsive words and actions as much as you do.

Tuesday of the 3rd Week of Lent #239

READING 1

"For We are Reduced, O Lord, Beyond Any Other Nation . . ." (Dn. 3: 25, 34-43).

Thought

One thing is evident: having the highest standard of living has not produced *the highest moral standard* of our nation.

When we as a nation exclude God and seek only material wealth, we surrender our high moral standards. We become weaker than the uninstructed pagans whom we imitate. Our nation can rightfully boast of its many fine churches and high count of membership in them. We can be proud that it has coins engraved with "in God we trust," but we cannot truthfully say we have any upsurge of honesty, unselfishness, or good moral conduct. In fact, these have reached an *all-time low*. As the Scriptures show us, there comes a time when both people and nation *go beyond the point of no return* and God's wrath comes down upon them.

Application

What we need is a complete devotion to God. We need an uncompromising loyalty to Christian principles. We need a zealous patriotism regarding the things on which our country was founded: liberty and justice for all. Let it begin with you and your family. *Rid yourself of race prejudices, bigotry, etc.*

Tuesday of the 3rd Week of Lent #239

GOSPEL

"Unless Each of You Forgives His Brother from His Heart . . ." (Mt. 18: 21-35).

Thought

Forgive seventy times seven times! It seems *we will never get a chance to hold a grudge!*

One feels admiration for the king who cancelled out the huge sum of money owed to him. No strings attached, no quibbling; out of compassion for the man he cancelled the debt . . . period! It is certainly not the way we tend to forgive. We impose conditions of apology or repentance: if you do this or that, *then I will forgive.* We overlook the fact that *to forgive is necessary for our own good* . . . whether it does the offender any good or not. "My heavenly Father will treat you *exactly* the same way each of you forgives his brother from his heart" (v. 35).

Application

Forgiveness takes on a different meaning when you realize your own future is at stake! Forgiveness never means that you have to like what somebody has done against you. It simply means that you have to forgive him, to be kind and helpful, to put the injury out of your mind, and not to take revenge . . . measure for measure . . . unless that is how you want God to treat you.

Wednesday of the 3rd Week of Lent #240

READING 1

"Teach Them to Your Children . . ." (Dt. 4: 1, 5-9).

Thought

Parents cannot train their children to go in one direction, and expect them to turn out well . . . *if they go off in another direction.*

It is true that parents cannot feel assured that their children will always follow what is being taught them, but they certainly have better odds for succeeding *if the example to follow is set for them at home.* It should not be "do as I say and not as I do." Most children's earliest ambition in life is to be like Mom and Dad. They copy and imitate as much as they can. The parents make an imprint, either good or bad, on the minds of their children that is hard to remove as they grow older.

Application

You will find a new respect in your own eyes as well as in the eyes of your children, if you teach them that obedience to God's laws always comes first. Your example will show them that there is not one set of rules for grown-ups and one for children. Use this Lent as a changing point in your life. Start moving in the direction that you want your children to move.

Wednesday of the 3rd Week of Lent #240

GOSPEL

"Whoever Fulfills and Teaches These Commands . . ."
(Mt. 5: 17-19).

Thought

The Commandments are not *restraints* upon our liberty; they are *safeguards* to keep us from hurting ourselves.

Cramming some food down a python's throat might be good for the snake, but *it is not the way to teach the commandments*. There are two ways to think of God's laws: one as a set of rigid, binding rules . . . like a whip that keeps lashing out with "thou shalt not," and the other as a set of directions that keep things in good running order for everyone concerned. We have sets of rules for the home, business, school, games, driving, etc. We know all the confusion we would have without them.

Application

We should not teach that God's laws are just "dos" and "don'ts" to make things hard for us. *Parents and teachers sometimes use this as* the only means *to emphasize the commandments. If* overdone *it only provokes a child to rebel against all laws, or to become a cowering weakling afraid to do anything on his own. If you stress the* advantages *of keeping them and* give a good example yourself, *you won't have to put so much stress on the* disadvantages *of breaking them.*

Thursday of the 3rd Week of Lent #241

READING 1

"Take Correction . . ." (Jer. 7: 23-28).

Thought

It is a lot easier to be *the one correcting* than to be the *object of correction.*

All of us are subject to correction. Correction is good for us. It keeps us "on our toes," keeps us from becoming too self-confident, and saves us from a lot of serious trouble later on. That is . . . *if we listen and pay heed to it.* Of course, correction does not always set too well with us. It may be quite painful and embarrassing. And even if we know someone is not being malicious with his correction, it is still not easy to take. *Undeserved criticism or correction deserves "looking into"* to see what we have innocently done to provoke someone to criticize.

Application

Being silent when you are corrected . . . deservedly or not . . . is certainly the ideal attitude. *However it does not mean giving "the silent treatment" that lets the other person know, and know it well, that you are unhappy about the situation. Humility and understanding, along with love of God, are the first steps toward conquering pride — the pride of thinking you are too good to be corrected.*

Thursday of the 3rd Week of Lent #241

GOSPEL

"Torn By Dissension . . ." (Lk. 11: 14-23).

Thought

Dissension is a *time waster* and a *disrupter* of more important matters . . . carrying out God's plans.

Some people carry "a chip on their shoulder" and go around most of the time just *daring somebody to knock it off*. The least little thing will cause dissension. They go around in a grouchy mood, poisoned by evil thoughts, just waiting to strike out like a snake at the first victim that crosses their path. They become narrow-minded like the Pharisees, bitter, and wholly out of contact with the Christian principles *they proclaim to uphold on Sunday*. That type of person can upset the whole household and *draw attention from God to himself . . . if you let him do so.* Instead of getting peeved and resentful, be charitable and have compassion on him. He needs pity. Look at the facts as honestly as you can and see if you are doing anything to add to his mood. Perhaps your attitude is irritating and over-bearing. Try hard to see if you can make the situation more tolerable.

Application

If you are the one with the "chip on your shoulder" get busy knocking it off yourself *before you destroy yourself altogether. Each days brings a new start. You do not have to remain in the same old rut. With a little effort you can start changing. Force yourself to smile. Hold back those mean words and say kind things.*

Friday of the 3rd Week of Lent #242

READING 1

"LET HIM WHO IS PRUDENT KNOW THEM . . ." (Hos. 14: 2-10).

THOUGHT

A nail is something like the prudent man . . . it gets involved only as far as the head will let it.

Prudence is wisdom applied to what you are *doing* and being ever mindful of the *consequences of your actions*. In other words, it deals in good old "common sense" in judging the things around you. You know when you have gone far enough; when you should quit or when you should get up more steam. It distinguishes between what is beneficial and what is harmful; what is good and what is bad. But it does not end with just *knowing;* it follows through with *doing what is right* and *not doing that which is wrong*.

APPLICATION

"Rose-colored glasses" are fine for brightening your outlook, but they sure mess up reality. *View things prudently; face them as they are.* Drop that which will harm you and hold on to that which will help you.

Friday of the 3rd Week of Lent #242

GOSPEL

"You Shall Love Your Neighbor As Yourself . . ." (Mk. 12: 28-34).

Thought

Loving your neighbor is not something *you do to be pleased* by the results; it is something done in which the results *will be pleasing to God.*

Love my neighbor as myself? Sometimes I wonder if I love myself! I feel disgusted and upset with the hasty, impulsive way I acted, with the mean words I've said. And I can grumble, be ungrateful and grouchy . . . but I still go on feeding myself, dressing myself, trying to make me happy. With this comparison in mind, it makes us realize that loving our neighbor has nothing to do with our own feelings and emotions, or even whether or not we like everything he does. It deals directly with *what we are supposed to do for him.* How he *reacts* is not to be considered in our part of the doing.

Application

Put aside your feelings and do kind things for somebody who is not kind to you. If he upsets you, recall the many times you upset yourself but still did things for yourself. Improving your attitude toward your neighbor *is something you can learn, but* don't expect gratitude *to be given in return as your* motive *for doing it.*

Saturday of the 3rd Week of Lent #243

READING 1

"In Their Affliction, They Shall Look For Me . . ." (Hos. 6: 1-6).

Thought

We often *turn to God* in our afflictions and just as often *turn away* when the *emergency has passed.*

Why must I suffer this affliction? It may be that God is bringing out of your suffering *results so wonderful* that they are worthwhile even at that price. *You may have been too busy before to even think about Him.* A serious illness often brings us to our senses; makes us realize that the material things we sought after are a lot of nonsense. It gives us an insight into our inner-selves. We see our faults and failings and the time we have wasted. We think of the many charitable things we should have done, should have said, but didn't. And we think . . . if we could just get well again *we would be different;* we would right all those things we failed to do. But it is not always so. We forget. When good health returns, the mind quickly turns back to depending upon man again. God is put on the shelf until the next emergency arises.

Application

When good health is given back to you after a severe illness, think of it as a new beginning, *a new chance to use all those opportunities you failed to use before. Make more out of your life now for God and for those around you.* Do not put God on the shelf. *He belongs there in your heart constantly . . . always.*

Saturday of the 3rd Week of Lent #243

GOSPEL

"ONE WAS A PHARISEE, THE OTHER A TAX COLLECTOR . . ." (Lk. 18: 9-14).

THOUGHT

The main difference between the Pharisee and the tax collector is the fact that the one was telling *how much God needed him* and the other *how much he needed God.*

Some, like the Pharisees, have the *kind of faith in themselves that others have in God.* Their prayer starts out with "I thank Thee" but the rest of it congratulates themselves and censures others for not doing as well. Pleased with themselves, thankful for themselves, they think of themselves as being so self-sufficient that *they really need nothing God or man can give.* They make it plain how much *God needs them* to set the world aright. And in their pride of spiritual attainment they look down upon all others. They go home and *continue* in their sinful self-righteous ways. But some, like the tax collector, realize they are sinners before God and man. They are dissatisfied with themselves and *know they need God.* And in spite of their many faults and sins, *they do not lose heart and quit praying.* They come to church to pray; to seek the help which *only God can give* and *will give.* They go home with a determination to do better and to sin no more.

APPLICATION

A humble man is not a hypocrite who rattles off a lot of faults he really does not think he has. He is one who forms a true estimate of himself. He recognizes the fact that when he does well it is because of God and not of his own doing. *And when he sins it is* because of his own doing; *he has turned away from God. YOU NEED GOD! Ask for His help.*

4th Sunday of Lent, Cycle A #31

READING 1

"Do Not Judge From His Appearance . . ." (1 Sm. 16: 1, 6-7, 10-13).

Thought

Outward appearance *has its importance* in living, but it should be *a reflection of that which you are inside.*

First impressions do carry a lot of weight, but we are sometimes apt to judge unfairly by that standard. Things are not always as they first appear to be. We even *bank on that "first impression"* we make on people so much, that we think of it as an allurement, an aid to help push through some projects we have in mind. We act as if we can put our good character "off and on" at will. And we sincerely hope *not to be caught* in our "off duty" moments. Of course, it usually does not take long for others to discover "the real YOU" inside. Character is more than skin deep. All that dazzling paraphernalia might make the outside look good, but it seldom "soaks in" to *improve the inside.*

Application

We should be *concerned about the impressions we make on others, but not for the purpose of "hoodwinking" them into thinking we are different from what we* really *are. Be determined to be what you want people to think you are by that first impression. But do not be so taken up with* the outward impression *you are making on people that you* neglect the inward impression you are making on God.

4th Sunday of Lent, Cycle A #31

READING 2

"TAKE NO PART IN VAIN DEEDS DONE IN DARKNESS; RATHER, CONDEMN THEM . . ." (Eph. 5: 8-14).

THOUGHT

"That's the way the ball bounces" may be true, but *you do not have to help it bounce* when there is question of a sin.

St. Paul told the Ephesians that just taking no part in works of darkness was not enough; they were to *condemn them also*. Too often we show indifference to the evil moral acts around us. Even if we do not take part in them, our silence seems to give consent. We are reminded *it is our duty* as Christians *to speak up and make clear our stand against sinfulness*. No matter how much the customs and times have changed, *we are all still subject to the laws of God*.

APPLICATION

In a time when the world seems to be "going to the dogs," it takes courage to stand up for your convictions, to refuse to take part in evil, to reprove those who do. No, we are not expected to jump up on a soap box and start "blasting away" with sermons about evil ways, but in our own circle of relatives and friends we have plenty of opportunities to speak up charitably. *Yes, you can expect jeers, spite, and scorn from some of them, but if you just save one soul it will have been worth it. And having a free conscience and living in the light of the Lord will certainly give you great comfort.*

4th Sunday of Lent, Cycle A

GOSPEL

"The Blind Man . . ." (Jn. 9: 1-41).

Thought

A person who makes a habit of walking around in the darkness is *bound to be tripped up by something.*

How different things look in the darkness. The same thing, such as a tree, that gives us comfort with its shade in the sunlight takes on a menacing frightening appearance at night. Or a dangerous bog along the side of the road, which we would certainly avoid in the light, takes on the appearance of an inviting picnic ground. Sin viewed in the light of grace looks so menacing that *we want to avoid it.* We want no part of it! But when we plunge into the darkness of sin, all the frightening conditions are disguised; evil takes on an alluring appearance. We are in "over our heads" before we even realize it. The natural condition of our eyes rebels and tries to give us warning. When we leave the light and plunge into a darkened area, we find it difficult to adjust at first. Everything becomes black for a few seconds. We are uneasy. Yet if we persist and stay in it for awhile, we become accustomed to it and *think* we do fairly well. But there is always uncertainty. We are never quite sure of anything.

Application

Just as when the eyesight is impaired the whole body suffers because of it, so it is that spiritual blindness causes the whole man to suffer. It wraps the human mind in its own blanket of darkness. False knowledge, ignorance, and uncertainty cloaks our every action so that we can no longer distinguish right from wrong. But you do not have to remain in spiritual blindness . . . sin. You can throw off the blanket of impairment at will by confession.

4th Sunday of Lent, Cycle B　　　　　　　　　　　　　　#32

READING 1

"UNTIL THE ANGER OF THE LORD AGAINST HIS PEOPLE WAS SO INFLAMED THAT THERE WAS NO REMEDY . . ." (2 Chr. 36: 14-17, 19-23).

THOUGHT

Justified anger should always be the *last resort* . . . not the first resort.

God used every method and means possible to get the people to change and always he *stressed compassion*. When everything of a more peaceful nature had been tried and nothing worked, He resorted to anger. How different we are. We are more apt to fly into a rage and *try the most drastic measure first* . . . ANGER! We sometimes . . . but not always . . . have compassion *after* we have lost our temper, hurt somebody, and in general made a mess of things. But that compassion is often more of the *selfish type*. We feel like a heel. We cannot stand to see the other person cry. It is the reaction that *hurts us* more so than the mean words bothering our conscience and making us feel sorry for the deed. In fact, if the person did not carry on like that, we would probably keep sounding off for awhile, and would not be one bit concerned about the hard feelings we are causing.

APPLICATION

Justified anger is sometimes the only means to remedy a situation, but not until all other measures have been tried *should it be used. And then, only with* the thought of helping somebody . . . not hurting. *One way of knowing if your anger was justified is the fact that no ill will lingers on. You have said what was to be said and then let the matter go. If your anger is more of the automatic "fast draw" type, try to develop a "quick trigger" follow-up of I AM SORRY along with it. Pray for the person.*

4th Sunday of Lent, Cycle B   #32

READING 2

"Faith . . . This Is Not Your Own Doing, It Is God's Gift . . ." (Eph. 2: 4-10).

Thought

Faith is a gift from God and what we do with it *shows our appreciation* or our lack of it.

A true gift is something freely given; it has nothing to do with whether we deserve or earn it. And the *thought behind the gift* as well as the *thought about the gift* is the real measure of its value. Faith, like any other gift, may be *used or ignored*. Think of how we react to our material gifts and you will see it also applies to our spiritual gifts. Some we barely acknowledge, some we toss in the waste basket at once, some we re-wrap and give to others, some we put on the shelf thinking we will use them later on (but never do), and some we put into use right away. We profusely offer thanks for the gift. The more we use the gift, the more we appreciate its value. We treasure it so much that we use it with tender care so that we can preserve it for future generations.

Application

It is tragic how little we appreciate our faith; *how little we give of our time and talents to develop this priceless gift. It is never too late to start showing your appreciation. Attend Mass more often. Spend some time in private prayer and spiritual reading.* Prove to God that you DO appreciate this precious gift of faith that He has given to you. *DO IT THIS LENT!*

4th Sunday of Lent, Cycle B #32

GOSPEL

"God So Loved the World That He Gave His Only Son, That Whoever Believes in Him May Not Die But May Have Eternal Life . . ." (Jn. 3: 14-21).

Thought

"Believes in Him" does not mean merely *assent of the mind to a creed* but *assent of the heart to Jesus.*

God's love is too vast to be put into words. The power of His love is above and beyond the change and decay of time; it is eternal. But powerful as it is, it cannot be fulfilled until we *respond* to it. *Not even a divine love can save us if we refuse to accept it.* Sin and unbelief keep us from being saved. They give proof of our refusal. It is not so much our unworthiness and sinful condition that God is concerned about. What He desires most is that we turn to Him to find relief and a solution to any problems we might have. There is not one person in the world who has not been *provisionally covered to be saved.* No one is beyond hope. But like an insurance policy, *unless you pay the premiums* you cannot expect any *dividends* or keep the policy in force. (Unless you obey God's laws you cannot expect the grace of keeping your faith in condition to help you.)

Application

The fact that God loves us so much that He was willing to give His only Son to die for us . . . should be so impressive that even the most disheartened person should take courage and feel loved. *Every sick person, every brokenhearted person, every man, woman, and child on earth that is hungry or suffering* has all of God's attention. *HE LOVES YOU!*

4th Sunday of Lent, Cycle C #33

READING 1

"THE MANNA CEASED. NO LONGER WAS THERE MANNA FOR THE ISRAELITES . . ." (JOS. 5: 9, 10-12).

THOUGHT

God's promise to *provide* for our needs never relieves us of the *responsibility of going out and gathering them up.*

There comes a time in the life of every living creature when it is expected to provide for its own needs. Even the small birds and animals of the forest are provided for by the parents until a certain time. Then they are pushed out into the world on their own. By instinct *they know their young would be handicapped unless they acquire the ability to care for themselves.* We can learn a lesson from that. Do not handicap your own children by doing everything for them. They have to learn to be independent. All of us creatures tend to become lax and unmindful of the source of all our blessings when everything comes too easily for us. Sometimes, like the Israelites, we have to have hardships to drive us back to depending upon God to save us.

APPLICATION

God has placed all of us in an environment necessary for us to acquire our needs. But He expects us to use our abilities and opportunities and not just sit and wait for things to come to us. This is true of the soul as well as of the body. We need to learn to be aggressive in discovering and acquiring the things that nourish and strengthen our soul. Seek ways to become closer to God.

4th Sunday of Lent, Cycle C #33

READING 2

"If Anyone Is in Christ, He Is a New Creation . . ."
(2 Cor. 5: 17-21).

Thought

The fact that a person has been a Christian all his life does not necessarily mean *he is living his life in Christ.*

Through faith all of us can be reconciled to God and begin to live a new life in Him. But that life in Christ should be a new life . . . *completely different from the old life without him.* It does not mean that we will have a new complete understanding about everything, but it points us in the direction that *gives meaning to all we do.* We are no longer just stumbling around in the dark. We know the *goal* toward which we are moving. We have a new feeling of *partnership with God* . . . but one that *gives him full control of our life.* Honesty in business, holding no grudges, faithfulness in marriage, and overcoming drunkenness, gluttony, and loose living are all necessary parts of this new life.

Application

Without God, without some all-encompassing unity *in all we do, life does not make sense. WE NEED GOD. We need this transformation . . . this new creation in our life. But to keep the newness we cannot be satisfied standing still. We have to keep changing, keep growing, adding to that which we have and are doing now.* Just putting in an hour a week with God on Sunday is not enough. *He "puts in" and "puts up" with us 24 hours a day. Take home a message from the Scripture readings and from the sermons and really try to apply it to your way of living all week long. Increase your prayers, your spiritual reading, and your kindness to others.*

4th Sunday of Lent, Cycle C #33

GOSPEL

"For Years Now I Have Slaved For You . . ."
(Lk. 15: 1-3, 11-32).

Thought

A person who thinks of work done for his family as "slaving" has no real love of them.

A slave seldom gains any recognition. Perhaps it is because of his *attitude* toward the work he is doing. Diligence and pride in his work are not there. He just does it to get it done. He has no real love or loyalty to his master. Much too often the attitude toward *your* work, particularly done for the family, becomes somewhat like the elder son's. YOU ARE THE SLAVE! You think the family takes you for granted. They seldom show any gratitude for your many hours of drudgery. Which may be true. But that *self-pity,* probably more than anything else, will be the main cause of your *heartaches.* Do not let the toilsome, monotonous, thankless everyday tasks be obstructions in seeking a holy life. *Let them be the means to draw you closer to God.*

Application

When you grumble and groan as you sweat under the stress and strain of working, you are turning God's service into the devil's service. *Think of yourself as helping to keep God's work going on earth . . . which you are doing, of course. Accept your tasks cheerfully. The sweating is all right . . .* but cut out the grumbling and groaning.

Optional Mass,* the 4th Week of Lent #244

READING 1

"Though I Sit in Darkness, the Lord Is My Light . . ." (Mi. 7: 7-9).

Thought

No one has to sit in the darkness as long as he is *near the light switch* . . . God.

Somebody is always telling us things look dark; conditions are not good for doing this or that. But then, things never have been perfect or never will be for everyone. Times are as good or as bad *as you make them.* If you are *content* to dwell in them and not improve them, they will remain as they are. But if you are *determined to change them,* you will. At least give it a try. The biggest problem is that most of us have no *real goal.* Yes, we say Heaven is our goal, but we drift aimlessly and avoid all the exertion we possibly can. A football player knows that standing still, looking at the goal post won't help him one bit. If he does not *take off* and start running towards it, *he will never get there.* If he is brought down along the way, he picks himself up and takes off again . . . at the next opportunity.

Application

Lack of interest and planning are the essential parts of failure. Do not let them be your downfall in your faith. Do not be content sitting in the dark. TURN GOD ON AND KEEP HIM ON. Have some type of plan in mind to renew and increase your effort. Set your goals high . . . but feasible . . . for attaining Heaven.

---

*This Mass may be used on any day of this week, especially in years B and C when the gospel of the man born blind is not read on the Fourtn Sunday of Lent.

Optional Mass,* the 4th Week of Lent #244

GOSPEL

"Ask Him. He is Old Enough to Speak For Himself . . ." (Jn. 9: 1-41).

Thought

It is not always *courtesy* that allows someone to speak for himself; it could be *not wanting to get involved*.

"Getting involved" is one of the basic principles of our Catholic Faith. The complaint that non-Christians often make is that Christianity has no real concern for the brotherhood of man or for the welfare of the people as a whole. *There is too much of a gap between talking and practicing* . . . lots of action inside but very little outside. Some of the complaints are true. There are too many so-called intelligent Christians who do not have the least idea that they have any responsibility *to speak up* and *get involved in helping another person*. Aware of it or not, we *are* responsible for one another. We should let it show in our actions as well as our alms. We have to develop a talent for getting along with all people, show a sincere concern for everyone's problems, and display assurance in the face of adversity. And pray. Pray hard.

Application

There are times, in fact most of the time, when we should let others speak for themselves. But we may not relieve ourselves of the responsibility of taking care of them. We should be standing by ready to help them; to back them up if needed. Our silence could very well be a sign of selfishness. *We do not want to give up any of our free time . . . so we avoid any involvement.*

---

*This Mass may be used on any day of this week, especially in years B and C when the gospel of the man born blind is not read on the Fourth Sunday of Lent.

Monday of the 4th Week of Lent #245

READING 1

"I Am About to Create New Heavens and a New Earth . . ." (Is. 65: 17-21).

Thought

Under present conditions creating a new earth would not help for long; there would always be some who would *try to mess it up again.*

"There shall always be rejoicing and happiness . . ." (v. 18). The words of Isaiah give us encouragement and lift us up to the ideal which God wants us to reach. The only problem is we have *control of the elevator,* and we do not stay up there for long. *Most of our actions take place on the lower levels.* Earth's attraction has us in its clutches. God speaks of the moral and spiritual creation within us which will be regenerated and made anew. To be made anew would be a wonderful thing. Most of us would go along with that . . . as long as we could keep all the material things that we found so attractive before. So our new creation at present would be more like a patch on an inner tube. It is not the ideal condition but that *patch is very important.* At least it *repairs* something that would have been *discarded* before.

Application

There's still plenty of room on the "ground floor" for those who want to rise above their earthly possessions. The ideal thing would be to throw out the old way of life and start afresh, but for most of us that would be next to impossible. We are just not that far advanced in spiritual life to give up all attachment to things. But this Lent make an attempt to make some improvement in your spiritual life. Start saying the meal prayers with your family, say the rosary, read the Bible, and if you are not a daily Mass-goer, attend Mass more often.

Monday of the 4th Week of Lent #245

GOSPEL

"Unless You People See Signs and Wonders, You Do Not Believe . . ." (Jn. 4: 43-54).

Thought

An undeserved rebuke can cause more hurt than a deserved one . . . if we let it.

There seemed to be no reason for rebuking the man about asking for signs; he had not asked for any. He had only begged Jesus to come and cure his son. It was as if Jesus was *testing the royal official's belief for the benefit of others.* He gave us a good example of how we should act when we encounter a sharp word or a reproof. This man was not deterred at all by what the reprimand might *seem to be indicating.* He pushed aside the rebuke as if he did not hear it. Or if he heard it, he felt it did not apply to himself. *He knew he was innocent.*

Application

We are thrown into a frenzy even when we know we are innocently blamed for something. We get upset over what someone might be indicating. *Oh, that we had the wisdom* to refuse to be offended. *Do not be hurt by rebuke or ridicule. Suffer it silently for God's sake and make it a* source of grace instead of a source of sin.

Tuesday of the 4th Week of Lent #246

READING 1

"Once More He Measured Off a Thousand . . ." (Ez. 47: 1-9, 12).

Thought

Anyone can measure and lay out a plan but *not everyone can carry it out.*

Efficiency or success in any endeavor is not due to *accident*. It has taken determination, courage, and persistence to attain it; planning, knowing where you are going, and how you are going to get there. Mankind has probably never lived in times such as we have now. *Changes in almost every area of our lives* are taking place; radical changes in dress, art, music, transportation, government, and even in our practice of religion. *Stubborn rebellion for or against the old standards is not the answer.* Whether we approve or disapprove, we cannot ignore the trends; we cannot afford to become static or stagnant. The ability to re-evaluate, plan and adjust to new conditions are particularly important today.

Application

Computer technology and automation may have swept aside the traditional ways of thinking . . . but not good old common sense! To some things we should adapt ourselves, but in regard to others we should make a stand and refuse to tolerate them . . . such as abortion, immorality, lack of respect for authority, drugs, etc. Plan your life for God and then with determination LIVE YOUR PLAN.

Tuesday of the 4th Week of Lent #246

GOSPEL

"It Is the Sabbath, and You are Not Allowed to Carry That Mat Around . . ." (Jn. 5: 1-3, 5-16).

Thought

In keeping the Sabbath, more is needed than simply *not forgetting God on that day.*

One cannot help but wonder what would happen to us in this modern age if the Old Testament laws were still in force. No work of any kind was allowed on the Sabbath. The penalty was almost always death. If we fixed our leaky roof, unstopped the plumbing, or even shoveled snow off the driveway to get to Mass we would have been "goners." A man gathering a few sticks for his fire was stoned. That would either eliminate our outside barbecues or there would be an awful lot of us exterminated beneath a pile of rocks. The Pharisees would not allow even a good deed on the Sabbath; no more helping our neighbor fight the grass fire that threatens his house, no rushing someone to the hospital in an emergency. (Of course, that last "good deed part" might not affect *some of us who are not so apt to lend a helping hand anyway!*)

Application

All this unwarranted severity about the Sabbath missed altogether the point of having the Law . . . *which was to show respect to God, to use right judgment, and to have mercy and love towards our neighbor.* Attending Mass is the most important time of the week. *There is always a message from Mass for you to take home. How you carry out the message . . . with charity or severity . . . shows how* much importance you place on God, *and what his laws were meant to accomplish.*

Wednesday of the 4th Week of Lent #247

READING 1

"My Lord has Forgotten Me . . ." (Is. 49: 8-15).

Thought

If you fear you have been forgotten, look around you and *see how many you have forgotten.*

It may look like God has forgotten you in desperate times, but *he knows what is best for you.* He knows what can and will draw you closer to Him *if you co-operate.* God takes no delight in our human suffering, any more than we do. And as soon as its purpose has been accomplished, the suffering is removed. Even earth itself groans under the terrific storms and strain of nature; it looks as if God has set out to destroy it. But when the storm is over the earth adjusts and goes back to starting anew. Many times it is even more beautiful than it was before. While hope remains we can resist with all our might the unpleasant trials of life. But once they *befall us* we should *accept them from the hand of God,* and have no doubt that he has a good purpose in them for us.

Application

Hardness of your condition will not be made any easier by worrying and making the condition harder. *Forget yourself. Look around you and see if there are others you can help by making their burden a little easier.*

Wednesday of the 4th Week of Lent #247

GOSPEL

"I Cannot do Anything of Myself . . ." (Jn. 5: 17-30).

Thought

There's a difference between *dependence upon God* and sitting around and *not doing anything yourself.*

A person who depends upon God for everything is constantly aware that *God depends upon him to carry out the work assigned.* None of us have been assigned the job of "a loafer." There *never* comes a time in our life when we can say simply that we have done enough. We have all been given certain talents and are expected *to use them as long as we live.* Age and infirmities may *slow things down a little* but it does not put an end to all our talents. Do not dwell upon your infirmities, incapabilities, and unworthiness. If you are asked to do something, depend upon God and *get busy doing it.* He will make you into that which you have to be to complete the work.

Application

You cannot always be the best in everything . . . in fact some of us are never the best in anything regardless of how hard we try. There is always somebody who can show you up by "out-doing" you. Adjust to your inadequacies and just do the best you can for God. He will be pleased with any work you do for Him.

Thursday of the 4th Week of Lent   #248

READING 1

"For They Have Become Depraved . . ." (Ex. 32: 7-14).

Thought

God shows that even the most depraved can be *saved by petition*.

God is not fickle when He changes his mind about a seemingly lost soul because of our prayers of petition. He is showing us that no matter how depraved the outward appearance of some one's soul is . . . by man's standards . . . *we should persist in prayer*. We are never to judge a person to be beyond hope. That is God's business, not ours. There are many people around us who have not been trained in even the simplest rudiments of life and government, much less about God. We misjudge them by calling them lazy. We say they have no ambition and do not want to improve. Would you under the same conditions, if you lived in such poverty? They have no "past" worth looking back upon. They can foresee nothing in the "future" to look forward to. And certainly their "daily" plight gives them no inspiration to do better. So they rebel and cry out their complaints to their fellow man.

Application

Now, as in Moses' time, complaints of dissatisfaction are murmured against man first . . . then against God . . . if no help comes from man. It is up to all of us to do what we can. Not only pray for them and hand out charity, but find ways and means to help direct them in the right path. Give meaning and respect to their lives and they will want to improve *themselves.*

Thursday of the 4th Week of Lent #248

GOSPEL

"You have Set Your Hopes . . ." (Jn. 5: 31-47).

Thought

Setting your hopes is not the same thing as *sitting on your hopes*.

We sometimes have high hopes, new ideas, and great enthusiasm about doing something, but we smother them with doubts and uncertainties before they can even get started growing. Inspiration is God's part . . . carrying it out is your part. Set your hopes high but set a goal that is *feasible*. No one really achieves anything without having some goal in mind. And one good thing about "goal setting" is that you will have an *exacting incentive*; you will know *what you want* from each day and you will know *why you want it*. Make God your main goal. Hopes cannot be any higher than those that are in Him.

Application

When you feel hopeful and inspired by an idea, get busy carrying it out. Let it grow. At least give it a chance to see what develops. If you are not pleased with it, there is always time to pluck it out after it has started growing.

Friday of the 4th Week of Lent #249

READING 1

"Because He is Obnoxious to Us . . ." (Wis. 2: 1, 12-22).

Thought

We sometimes think people are *obnoxious* when they say something *contrary to what we believe.*

If the words of an obnoxious person disturb us to the point of getting us upset or angry enough to hold a grudge, it is a good idea *to look into what he has said.* There may be some *truth* in it. We just might have plenty of faults that need correcting. Restrain your imagination. Keep to the facts that really exist. Try to determine what it is you have said or done to make the person speak or act in that manner. If you find nothing; *forget about it.* Chalk it up to his bad mood. But if you find something; *work on it.*

Application

Conflicts of opinion are normal, but to make a "big deal" out of them is foolish. Some people have acquired the knack of expressing their opinions in an obnoxious way. They do not seem to know any other way of speaking. Why let them make you obnoxious in return? *It is far better strategy and better for your own disposition to be charitable and speak kind words in return. Make* being extra kind to them *one of your sacrifices for Lent.*

Friday of the 4th Week of Lent #249

GOSPEL

"Still, We Know Where This Man Is From . . ."
(Jn. 7: 1-2, 10, 25-30).

Thought

The things we know sometimes *can become obstacles* . . . particularly if it is not very much that we know.

Some of the people of Jerusalem *started to believe* in Jesus, but the *little bit of knowledge* they had held them back. "Stick-to-itiveness" is a good quality as long as *the thing to which you are sticking is worthwhile*. Even when the truth seems obvious, when a change seems to be in order, some will still cling tenaciously to the little bit of knowledge they have. They refuse to change. With flimsy reasoning and a closed mind, they argue themselves out of what they ought to believe in. The devil delights in our use of reasoning when it places *obstacles* in the way of our faith. The more knowledge we acquire about our religion, the more our faith will be deeply rooted. From time to time we should all pause and take a long, hard look at ourselves . . . to see what we are doing and how we are progressing.

Application

Have you appraised your own efforts lately in church? Are you convinced you have made the most of your opportunities to learn about the "updating?" Or are you clinging so tenaciously to all the "old ways" that they are becoming obstacles that are drawing you away from God?

Saturday of the 4th Week of Lent   #250

READING 1

"I Knew Their Plot Because the Lord Informed Me . . ."
(Jer. 11: 18-20).

Thought

Knowing someone is plotting an evil against us does not *lessen the hurt much*. It may even *increase* it.

We have all experienced to some degree a time when we knew of someone plotting an evil against us. We were innocent victims because we made some miscalculated remark or we unknowingly stepped on someone's toes. There was just nothing we could do about it. *And knowing about it did not make it any easier for us to accept.* The plotting hurt! And to make matters worse, we became so wrapped up in our hurt feelings that *entrusting our cause to God* (as the Scriptures tell us to do) *was the farthest thing from our mind.* In fact, we were so upset that we lashed out with searing words of anger that dealt out our own vengeance.

Application

If there is nothing that you can do about someone's evil scheme or malicious talk . . . just "grin and bear it" . . . the best you can. You are in good company. *Our Lord and many of the saints went through the same thing.* Oh, accepting and being a willing victim to someone's plotting is certainly not easy. *But willfully taking revenge against him will be a* lot harder to rectify with God. *Take the means to protect yourself from harm, but do not try to get even in revenge.*

Saturday of the 4th Week of Lent #250

GOSPEL

"Do Not Tell Us You Too have been Taken in! ..." (Jn. 7: 40-53).

Thought

To be "taken in" is not so bad if it *leaves you in a better situation afterwards.*

What someone else might title "being taken in" could very well be the best thing that ever happened to you. It all depends on who and what is taking you in. Certainly the Pharisees would have been *better off* if they had been "taken in" by the words of Jesus instead of persisting in their sinful ways. Of course, there is always a chance that someone is trying to "put something over on you" when you least expect it. You have to be careful and on guard for that. If you are a victim, do not let it bother you. Accept and make the best of it. As long as there is room to crawl out from under it there is no problem. *Humility gives you the room.* Sometimes you are in the wrong and need to get "shook up." "Being taken in" may just do that.

Application

The embarrassment, the feeling of dumbness of "being taken in" may grate upon your sensitive feelings, but nevertheless, you should not be so upset that you overlook the lesson that God has in it for you. The lesson does not need to be spelled out. *You do not have to understand fully its meaning in your life. It is enough to know that* there is a purpose in God allowing *it to happen. Learn from it, even if it is* to be more cautious about choosing those you trust.

5th Sunday of Lent, Cycle A #34

READING 1

"I Will Open Your Graves and
Have You Rise from Them . . ." (Ez. 37: 12-14).

Thought

Rising from the grave of death will not bring much comfort to those who die in grave sin.

Bring us back to life! If a man promised us that, we would probably not place much hope in his words. In fact, we would be more apt to think he was a "hopeless case" himself. But in this Scripture Reading we are not dealing with man's words; *we are dealing with God's.* What is humanly impossible is not impossible for God. There is no limit to what He can do. He who made us from nothing certainly will have no problem bringing us back from the grave.

Application

Rising from the grave of death will not give much hope unless you raise yourself from the grave of sin while living. Give yourself a new lease on life this Lent. Go to confession. And see if there are some elderly people around you who have no way of getting to church for confession. Take them along with you.

5th Sunday of Lent, Cycle A #34

READING 2

"Those Who are in the Flesh Cannot Please God . . ."
(Rom. 8: 8-11).

Thought

Man is certainly "in the flesh" but there is a difference between *being* "in the flesh" and *dwelling* "on the flesh."

Some have labeled this era "the fun age" . . . anything and everything goes in styles and actions. Immorality is "in" . . . morality is "out" . . . so some say. Yes, "anything goes" and it looks like *God was the first made to go.* It is evident, physically and spiritually, people have got rid of God or the world would not be in the mess it is in now. *A people without God is certainly on the way out* . . . out, away from Heaven. With so much emphasis nowadays, in the media of communication, on *pleasing the senses* it isn't easy not to pamper or *dwell on the body.* St. Paul tells us that when we let ourselves be controlled by the whims of the flesh, *we cannot please God.*

Application

Are we so weak and wishy-washy in our faith that we set aside God's standards and are "taken in" by styles and immoral actions of a godless few? Refusal to accept and take any part in them, and voicing your disapproval will soon put a stop to them. When the ethical standard is low, it should not take too much effort to raise it. A person may be on the very verge of doing evil, but a simple "NO" can put an end to it.

5th Sunday of Lent, Cycle A #34

GOSPEL

"Jesus Began to Weep . . ." (Jn. 11: 1-45).

Thought

Sympathy is best from a person who has *already gone through the same thing.*

The touching human sympathy Jesus showed by weeping over Lazarus should make us realize *how very tender His love is;* how very near He is when we also mourn our loved ones. He has suffered the grief of mourning a loved one. *He knows what you are going through.* Sorrow makes us think deeply, long, and soberly. It can be an opportunity to grow in faith, to inspire others, and to prove our love and trust in God. Martha and Mary proved their love. They turned at once to Jesus when they realized how sick their brother was. No doubt, they felt heartsick and puzzled over the delay of His coming, but they never lost confidence or doubted His love. Martha's words, "Even now, I am sure that God will give you whatever you ask of him" (v. 22), showed her faith.

Application

Turn to God in your deep sorrow. He understands. He cares. He will give you comfort. YOU DO NOT MOURN ALONE.

5th Sunday of Lent, Cycle B #35

READING 1

"I WILL MAKE A NEW COVENANT . . ." (Jer. 31: 31-34).

THOUGHT

A covenant, a promise, for some people, is honored only as long as it *goes along with what they want to do.*

The Old and New Covenants differ in several ways. The New Covenant was not to be just a set of rules like those which were given to Moses in the midst of thunder and flashing lightning — laws to be kept out of fear. In Moses' time most people thought of God as a far-off one whose only concern was about the laws being kept. They felt no personal desire to please Him; only fearful anxiety to do things to avoid punishment. All they learned about God was through chosen prophets — prophets who faithfully delivered God's message but could give no explanation of them. The New Covenant was to be no longer just an outward set of rules to be obeyed. It was to have laws written in the heart, *to be kept out of love for God.* And they were to be taught by the Son of God, who would take on our nature, who would make it clear that He would understand our every feeling. Here was a God so personal, so loving, so giving of His entire self that *no right thinking person could help but love him and want to do everything to please him.*

APPLICATION

Make this Lent different from all the other Lents. *Make a covenant with God* an agreement *to do some spiritual act* that will last all year long. *Perhaps an agreement to say certain prayers everyday . . . to read daily from the Bible or some spiritual book . . . to make the Stations of the Cross every Friday . . . to say the rosary . . . to attend an extra Mass during the week.* Prove you really love God enough to do something extra for him.

5th Sunday of Lent, Cycle B #35

READING 2

"HE LEARNED OBEDIENCE FROM WHAT HE SUFFERED . . ." (Heb. 5: 7-9).

THOUGHT

When we have not shown much obedience to God beforehand, it is not easy *to learn obedience when we are suffering.*

Many of us learn nothing from our suffering except the ability to groan, grumble, and make life pretty miserable for those around us. And we feel if there is any obedience to be learned, it is not on *our* part; it is *on the part of those waiting on us!* We are bound to experience irritability and selfish impatience when we make "ourself" the center of attention instead of God. Try to forget about yourself. Center your attention upon God and being pleasing to him . . . *by being pleasant to those around you.* It is never too late to learn obedience. It is possible, *if you are determined enough,* to give up your will to God and accept your suffering *even when you cannot rejoice* over what you are going through.

APPLICATION

When you are full of aches and pains with a chronic condition, and can no longer help yourself, your faith becomes the most important ingredient in your life. *But you cannot expect your faith to have much effect if you have not been using it all the time. Just throwing it in* as a last resort to see if it will work or not won't help much. *Like yeast in bread, it has to be mixed in beforehand with other things before it can produce the best results.* Start mixing it NOW with kindness toward others, faithfully attending Mass, saying prayers, doing charitable deeds, etc.

5th Sunday of Lent, Cycle B #35

GOSPEL

"WHILE THE MAN WHO HATES HIS LIFE IN THIS WORLD PRESERVES IT TO LIFE ETERNAL . . ." (Jn. 12: 20-33).

THOUGHT

There are a lot of people who hate their life in this world but won't necessarily get to Heaven.

If hating everything, including one's self, was the necessary condition for getting to Heaven some people *would have it made.* They are cynical and gripe about everything. Nothing you do can please them. They hate the way the Church is run, the government, the neighborhood, their job, their family . . . *you name it, they hate it.* This is not the kind of person Jesus was talking about. He was talking about the person who does not cling or have any undue attachment to his possessions on earth; who uses his earthly gifts as a means to draw him closer to God. And in times of tragedy . . . fire, storms, flood, financial set-backs . . . when all is wiped out, he does not feel despair. *He knows that his means of existence . . .God . . . is not gone and that life is worth living.* So he picks up the pieces and starts again, knowing that God will supply his needs just as he did before.

APPLICATION

God gives us everything we have on earth . . . but if we misuse them we will lose them. *We all have earthly possessions that we treasure highly and would find quite difficult* to give up. *We are not expected to give them up, to throw them aside.* It takes a saint to do that . . . *and God knows how few in number they are.* But He does expect you not to let the "possession" possess *you* and become a source of sin . . . pride and greed . . . instead of a means to draw you closer to Him.

5th Sunday of Lent, Cycle C   #36

READING 1

"Remember Not the Events of the Past, the Things of Long Ago Consider Not . . ." (Is. 43: 16-21).

Thought

A person who *lives in the past* cannot be paying much *attention to today.*

"Now, in the good old days things used to be different." How often we hear that phrase. No doubt, there is some truth in it, but one of the things that made those days so different . . . changed them into the "good old days" . . . is our *evaluation of them now.* All the thousands of annoyances and frustrations that bothered us then have been glossed over by the highlights *we choose to remember.* On the other hand, there are those who remember only the trials and sins of the past; *they do not consider those days good at all.* The thought of the past still plagues their mind and drags them down with worry. *They cannot see today's value for all their concern about yesterday.*

Application

Living with the past *is not the same as living* in the past. *What you have learned from the days gone by can help you, but hanging on to it, dwelling upon it so much that you* neglect today, *will only hinder you.* God has new things for you to do, new things for you to learn. CONCENTRATE ON TODAY *and live it for God.* Every day lived for God is a good day.

5th Sunday of Lent, Cycle C #36

READING 2

"My Entire Attention Is on the Finish Line . . ." (Phil. 3: 8-14).

Thought

There is no person who *strives faithfully* all his life to obtain "a sole aim" who does not *obtain it in some degree.*

Anyone who has run in a race knows that *looking back to see how well he is doing* only slows him down. If we want to win a race we have to keep our entire attention on the finish line. Never mind how things have turned out. That's all behind you. Do not look back. Push on ahead. Oh, there may be times when it seems you are running in a maze of barriers. And no matter how you push and pull, shove and yank, determined to get over them . . . they are still there. You may begin to wonder if you are ever going to reach the goal at all . . . *much less win the race.* Have confidence. God is your goal as well as *your source of energy.* All you have to do is ask Him for help.

Application

The only competitor you have is yourself. *St. Paul did not tell you that you were running* against *anyone else. So you are* bound *to win the race* as long as you keep moving toward Christ . . . *and not away from Him.*

5th Sunday of Lent, Cycle C #36

GOSPEL

"They Were Posing This Question to Trap Him . . ."
(Jn. 8: 1-11).

Thought

It is bad enough when innocent questions sometimes bring out answers that could trap a person; it is easier to answer those who *plan questions as booby traps* to hurt someone.

We are so flattered that someone asks us a question that we sometimes "throw all caution to the wind"; we become victims of guile and deceit. We may find questions about our faith are not always asked to obtain sincere information. They can be asked to trap us into embarrassing situations from which it is difficult to extricate ourselves. Jesus shows us in this Gospel how we should treat this kind of questioning. First, with silence; and then, if the questioning persists, we should choose our words carefully and judiciously. Without any display of anger, we are to turn the question around so that the *full responsibility for answering rests on the other person.* For example: "Why should you confess your sins to a priest?" Answer: "That's an interesting question. But why do you think I shouldn't?" Use this as an opportunity to demonstrate the power of your faith.

Application

If you find yourself confronted with sincere questions about your religion that are beyond your ability to answer . . . say so. But offer to find out the answers from your parish priest. *Or better yet, if one is truly interested in the Catholic Faith, offer to go with him to see the priest or attend a study group with him.* The review will be good for you.

Optional Mass,* 5th Week of Lent #251

READING 1

"He Found the Boy Lying Dead . . ." (2 Kgs. 4: 18-21, 32-37).

Thought

The *depth* of one's faith is not determined *by the emotion displayed.*

How different this scene of death is from the death of Lazarus. There is no crying, no display of emotion, no placing of the dead boy in a burial place, and seemingly no personal contact or pleading with Elisha at all. Just simply placing him on the bed of the man of God, walking out, closing the door, and letting him be found there. One is apt to think the mother was pretty cold-hearted and indifferent. But the important lesson, in both Readings today, is *the strong faith that was placed in God and complete acceptance of what had happened.*

Application

We all react differently with our emotions. Some become openly emotional about every little thing . . . *there is no doubt how they feel. And some of us keep our feelings* buried deep inside — *seldom brought to the surface. We suffer grief that the world never knows and burdens that the nearest never suspect. One should never judge another by the display or lack of emotion.*

---

*This Mass may be used on any day of this week in years B and C when the gospel of Lazarus is not read on the 5th Sunday of Lent.

Optional Mass,* 5th Week of Lent #251

GOSPEL

"Yet, After Hearing That Lazarus Was Sick, He Stayed on Where He Was For Two Days More . . ." (Jn. 11: 1-45).

Thought

Much too often we try to *explain away God's miracles* with human reasoning or logic.

If Jesus had come immediately when Lazarus had died, some would have said his friend was just sleeping. But after four days in the tomb there could be *no doubt* about the miracle. *Lazarus was raised from the dead by Jesus!* His hands and feet were bound individually with linen strips; and so he was able to walk out of the tomb after he was restored to life, even before he was untied. It is a tendency in fallen human nature to doubt everyone and everything . . . including the miracles of God. Some attribute nothing to Him until all logical reasons have been explored. And even then, some, with a shrug of the shoulder, still do not believe God had any part in it. *Nothing is beyond God's power.* He can do all things. He is not limited to man's standards.

Application

Occasionally we still hear of miracles. People the doctors have given up are miraculously cured. A strange phenomenon of nature kills all but one person. Etc. We are astonished and awed by the event. We get all wrapped up in every little detail. So wrapped up, that we may overlook the message in it — a message that reveals God's power and glory and should be the source of drawing us closer to Him. If you think you need a miracle in your life . . . ask God for it . . . but accept whatever way He chooses to answer your prayer . . . *or not answer it directly.*

---

*This Mass may be used on any day of this week in years B and C when the gospel of Lazarus is not read on the 5th Sunday of Lent.

Monday of the 5th Week of Lent #252

READING 1

"Are You Such Fools . . . To Condemn a Woman of Israel Without Examination and Without Clear Evidence?" (Dn. 13: 1-9, 15-17, 19-30, 33-62).

Thought

Suspending judgment of your neighbor until an evil story has at least been proved *is wise.* But *passing no judgment at all is the wisest.*

Before we even ask ourselves whether an evil story about someone is true or false, we have a tendency to *start believing the worst.* We become stand-offish and give him the cold shoulder; not condemning him . . . but *being on guard.* We put two and two together, so we think, and even his innocent good actions suddenly take on an evil dimension. We all know the hurt that was felt when an untrue rumor about ourselves got back to us. There was *some grain of truth* in it but so *minute,* so twisted out of proportion that we could hardly recognize it. But there was enough truth to start tongues wagging and cause a feeling of distrust from those whom we trusted and we thought knew us better.

Application

The tongue, as well as the ear, can be a source of pollution. *Slander is a terrible, spreading disease that* contaminates *everyone it touches . . . unless you make yourself* immune *to it.* Ignore the evil story. *Be charitable. When someone is being slandered he needs a friend. Be that friend. Judgment is for God, not man.*

Monday of the 5th Week of Lent, Cycles A and B   #252

GOSPEL

"Nor Do I Condemn You . . ." (Jn. 8: 1-11).

Thought

Man judges from the *past*. God judges from the *present*.

The first Reading dealt with a false accusation, the Gospel deals with an accusation that was true. We can see in either case we have no right to judge or condemn. This by no means indicates we should *tolerate* or *accept* the evil practices of someone. *It is our duty to speak out against them.* But our speaking out disapproval does not mean we are to set ourselves up as condemning judges. We have all done things in the past that we wish we had not done. We are sorry. We would like to just forget it. Our own experience shows us that because a person has sinned once does not mean he will always sin. *People have been known to change over night.*

Application

How different, how much more merciful God is than man. God does not stress the past. It is the present, the future He is interested in. If you are sorry for a sin, confess it and let it go. Show the same attitude toward someone else who is sorry for his sin. LET HIS SIN GO AS WELL AS YOUR OWN.

Monday of the 5th Week of Lent, Cycle C #252

GOSPEL

"You are Your Own Witness . . ." (Jn. 8: 12-20).

Thought

If you cannot testify with assurance about *your own actions,* your testifying *about another's* won't give much assurance either.

Being your own witness, standing face to face with yourself, *knowing in your own conscience you are right,* regardless of the false testimony of others is more important than the testimony of dozens of others *coming to your rescue.* When you *know* you have done the right thing, you will not be disturbed by a witness to the contrary. Oh, you might feel "shook-up" at the surprising turn of events; that is only human. And it may take a little time, with many heartaches, but you can endure it with patience. TRUTH WILL ALWAYS WIN OUT.

Application

You cannot expect to win the confidence and support of others if you are not sincere and honest in dealing with facts. *Live your life in a manner that your words will be accepted at "face value."* A shady character *makes an interesting plot for a* movie, *but it is a* characteristic we can do without in real life.

Tuesday of the 5th Week of Lent   #253

READING 1

"WITH THEIR PATIENCE WORN OUT BY THE JOURNEY, THE PEOPLE COMPLAINED . . ." (Nm. 21: 4-9).

THOUGHT

The time for making *a reasonable complaint* is certainly not when you are *impatient and beyond reason yourself.*

Impatience is *contagious.* Our moodiness, our "out-of-sorts" provoking words are sometimes more *infectious* to those around us than a wrong doing. It has a way of rubbing off on all those we contact. When we are tired we say things and make outrageous complaints that we would never make when we are rested. And of course, matters become worse when everyone *starts complaining back to us!* The best thing to do is to *keep quiet when you are worn out* . . . which is easier said than done. Who cares about the *best thing* when we are feeling in the *worse mood!* But at least give it a try. And if you do "sound off" and "put your foot in your mouth" with mean hasty words, it is a lot easier . . . while you have your foot there . . . *to stomp on your pride and say you are sorry right away.* It will certainly help to ease matters a bit.

APPLICATION

We usually think of patience only in connection with not getting angry or flaring up. It is also necessary at times when the weather turns out bad and spoils your plans, when a headache or illness keeps you home and makes you cranky, when friends and the family disappoint you, etc. Opportunities for practicing patience are all around you. Your daily living is just full of them . . . if you want to use them as sources of grace instead of aggravation.

Tuesday of the 5th Week of Lent #253

GOSPEL

"Since I Always Do What Pleases Him . . ." (Jn. 8: 21-30).

Thought

It is not enough to live a life so that God can *tolerate us*; we should live a life so that God will be *pleased with us.*

If we always try to do what pleases God the *results are bound to be pleasing.* The problem is we want to "put the cart before the horse." We are usually more interested in the prospects of the *results being pleasing to us* before we tackle anything. So, since we cannot forget ourselves completely, we should *use our self-interest and talents as a means of proving to God that we have not forgotten Him.* Develop these talents and interests in a way that they will be a source of grace. If you like stamp collecting share your duplicates with the missions. Art work can help raise money for church. Wood work and sewing can do the same, as well as being a godsend for your pastor who needs help with various repair jobs and supplies for the altar. Pleasing God does not take brilliance and a lot of education. It takes *faith, action, and common sense.* Do not be concerned if you have only little things in which you can please God. *In His measure they are big things.*

Application

Wishful thinking and day dreams about pleasing God are all right . . . if you are planning on just standing there looking up to Heaven. *But you will have a better chance of actually getting there if you* change your wishbone into backbone *with persistent determination and positive action.*

Wednesday of the 5th Week of Lent #254

READING 1

"Blessed Be the God of Shadrach, Meshach, and Abednego . . ." (Dn. 3: 14-20, 91-92, 95).

Thought

A truth that angers someone when it is stated may be the very instrument through which God will draw that person to Himself.

We hesitate sometimes about standing up for our convictions; *we do not want to stir up a "hornet's nest."* But in reality, we are more of a *coward* and do not want to *suffer the consequences of someone's wrath.* So we take the easy way out. We override the dictates of our conscience and *give in* to avoid trouble. It is one thing to know the truths about God and another to express them when we are forced to make a choice between God and man. What a good example these three young men gave us! Not only did they express their convictions, but they made no demands, and showed no concern about their own safety. The words, ". . . may he save us! But even if he will not . . ." (v.18), showed they were willing to stand up for their faith and *leave the results up to God.*

Application

Do not worry about objections in discussing your religion. In many cases the only reason a person raises an objection is that something you have said has sparked his interest. STAND UP FOR YOUR RELIGION, but be prepared as much as possible to answer objections. This may be the ground work for a conversion.

Wednesday of the 5th Week of Lent #254

GOSPEL

"AND THE TRUTH WILL SET YOU FREE . . ." (Jn. 8: 31-42).

THOUGHT

You have to make a *commitment* to the truth before it can *set you free*.

The truth about anything certainly *does free us* in our conscience; it also frees us of the *uncertainty* about things. But this is not the truth Jesus was talking about. He was talking about a spiritual truth concerning God, sin, and eternal life. He did not say that sin and temptation would be eradicated by this truth; that there would be no more of them in your life. He was saying that if you really try to live according to His teaching, the power of evil can be broken; it can be conquered by a simple "NO." You do not need someone else to make you a slave. *You can be in bondage to your own self;* wrapped up so much in your own sinful ways that you virtually become a slave to your own body.

APPLICATION

You do not have to be a "slave to sin" unless you want to be. *The* more *you say NO to yourself the* easier *it becomes to say NO to the devil and his temptations. The* more *you say YES to God the* easier it becomes *to say YES to whatever He asks of you.*

Thursday of the 5th Week of Lent #255

READING 1

"I WILL MAINTAIN MY COVENANT . . . THROUGHOUT THE AGES . . ." (Gn. 17: 3-9).

THOUGHT

Our covenants barely cover the situation for a *brief time* much less "throughout the ages."

That is quite a covenant that covers *all the descendants down through the ages!* And how simple our part is in keeping it. All we have to do is *recognize God as our God.* When we make a covenant we have so many stipulations, added requirements that we demand to be kept, that they over-shadow the covenant itself. *They are really more of a hardship than an aid.* And woe to the one who does not keep his part! We never want to trust him again. A second chance is out! *There is no such thing as charity for the guy who cannot keep his end of the bargain.* Now if it is *our part that is faltering* . . . that is another story. We can find all kinds of plausible excuses and expect *no limit to mercy and forgiveness.*

APPLICATION

If God reacted as we do, we would all be lost. A covenant is between at least two persons who have come to an agreement. *It is not just one imposing a lot of demands upon another. It is a "give and take" situation on both sides. And without charity, love, and understanding no covenant can ever be kept in any degree at all. Be considerate and lenient when someone falters with his end of the bargain. Give him a chance to redeem himself.* Make sure that you are keeping your part with God in his covenant with you.

Thursday of the 5th Week of Lent #255

GOSPEL

"If A Man Is True to My Word
He Shall Never See Death . . ." (Jn. 8: 51-59).

Thought

Scientific study has helped to *increase* man's life span but not to *prolong it eternally* . . . only God can do that.

To "never see death" — just for being true to His Word! *That alone should attract us to God.* But how can this be? We see evidence of death all around us. The flowers decay; a dead tree falls; a bird, an animal lies in death alongside the road. Some of our loved ones no longer walk with us on earth. And our body, so we are told, even while living is in a perpetual process of dying cell by cell. We know from centuries of experience *everything eventually does see death.* Yet Jesus said: "If a man is true to my word he shall never see death" (v. 51). It is evident it is not the death of the body itself of which He is speaking. *It is the death of the soul.* We are promised an immortal life that has no time-boundaries; a supernatural life of the spirit that cannot be terminated by pain, hardship, or death. It cannot be affected by earth's trials *unless we let it be.*

Application

We do not have to understand the mystery of how this life can be immortal. It is enough to know that God promised it to us. If we are true to His Word we will be eternally with Him in Heaven. But we cannot be true to anything until we try to learn all we can about it. *Never be satisfied with what you know about God.* Continue to increase your knowledge.

Friday of the 5th Week of Lent　　　　　　　　　　#256

READING 1

"IN THEIR FAILURE THEY WILL BE PUT TO UTTER SHAME . . ."
(Jn. 20: 10-13).

THOUGHT

The only time we have to worry about "failure" is *when we do not keep God on our side.*

One might say: "That is easy to say, 'Do not worry about failure.'" But when you have a family to feed, a house to pay for, and bills coming in regularly, and *everything depending upon your success* . . . you DO WORRY ABOUT FAILURE! Yes, failure certainly does have an effect upon us. Sometimes when we fail, the confusion in our mind makes us not sure of which way to turn. We cannot understand what happened. We had put forth our best effort. We had sized up the situation from all angles and still everything turned out wrong. But *wrong by whose measure?* OUR'S or GOD'S? God tests the just in success as well as failure. Perhaps *failure* was the only way to shake us out of our "contented unproductive rut," to prepare us for *better things*. Many a person has bounced back from what would be termed as complete failure to make a successful life beyond his fondest dreams. Never mind how things turn out. *You are a failure only when you give up trying.* God expects you to *work on the cause*; He *works on the result*.

APPLICATION

God has a message *in your failures. But if you dwell upon them too long or overly much, you are not looking for a message there. YOU ARE LOOKING FOR SELF-PITY! Pick up the pieces and start again. At least you* learned how not to do something. *Trust in God's wisdom. He knows what He is doing.*

Friday of the 5th Week of Lent #256

GOSPEL

"Scripture Cannot Lose Its Force . . ." (Jn. 10: 31-42).

Thought

The strength of the Scriptures can be *diluted* in practice, but *the text retains its force.*

No matter how or in what way some try to interpret, change, or "chop away" at the Scriptures to fit in with their own designs and craving, *it remains the same.* It does not lose its force because someone objects to it, preaches it differently, or publishes a "far-out" meaning in a book. Down through the ages there have been many changes made in Church discipline . . . updating by the Church . . . to fit in with the times in which we live. But in no way has it changed the force of the Scriptures. Some, like the Jews in this Gospel, have so completely *rejected the accidental changes* in the Church that it has *embittered and alienated them from the true faith.* Apparently they will believe in a religion only so long as it *follows a pattern they know.* They have never done anything different in all those years. They can see no reason to change now. "What was good enough for my ancestors is good enough for me" . . . so the saying goes . . . *and so goes their faith!*

Application

That deep-rooted prejudice has passed on down through the ages with many an unwise man. To hang on to a traditional way of doing things merely because you have never done otherwise *is no reason not to make a* change. *Maybe the changes seem to be confusing to you, but one thing comes through clearly, more and more of our leaders are talking about how to know, love, and serve God better* through our fellowman. *Be patient. Try to see God's purpose in these changes.* You cannot go wrong if you go along with the Pope.

Saturday of the 5th Week of Lent #257

READING 1

"I Will Deliver Them from All Their Sins of Apostasy..." (Ez. 37: 21-28).

Thought

Who would dare to try to *save* a godless and impenitent person who seems *beyond hope? God would* . . . and He expects *our help*.

Apostasy means "forsaking or abandoning what one has once professed." We all know someone who has "fallen away," forsaken his Faith and seemingly gone from bad to worse. We've prayed for him for years but still he remains indifferent. At times he is downright sarcastic towards our attempts. We feel like "giving up" on him. But in the Scriptures today God gives us hope. "I will deliver them from all their sins of apostasy . . ." v. 23). NEVER GIVE UP HOPE FOR ANYONE. No one is beyond hope as long as he has a breath of life. And even beyond that last breath keep praying for him. We never know what one's last thoughts may be. It is not necessary for us to see with our own eyes someone return to his Faith. *Grace can work without us knowing it.* The mercy of God is far beyond our limits.

Application

In your zeal to save someone you would like to jump right in and blast away with reproof, *but that is certainly not the best approach.* Prayer, gentle reproof *backed by your good example, and occasionally* inviting him to church . . . *then dropping the subject if refusal is encountered . . . will be more beneficial.* A nagging, condemning attitude only *stirs up a defensive, antagonistic response. Keep praying for him. God will answer your prayers if he is worthy of being saved.*

Saturday of the 5th Week of Lent #257

GOSPEL

"He Withdrew Instead . . ." (Jn. 11: 45-57).

Thought

Withdrawing to take advantage of a more ideal *opportunity* for discussion at a later date is a sign of *wisdom, not cowardice.*

There is a time *for standing up for your convictions* and there is *a time to withdraw;* a time when it is not only useless, but it would make matters worse to continue to make your stand. There is *no sense making a heroic stand over trifles,* particularly when you encounter someone who is unreasonable. It might make a wide, uncomfortable gap over which there can be no future communications. Perhaps in good conscience, you cannot "give in" one bit. The *issue is important,* but tempers are already flaring up. The sensible thing to do is circle around the situation with the famous politician's remark: "That's an interesting point." Then graciously *withdraw until the atmosphere is not so tense.* Discuss the subject later. You will obtain better results for God.

Application

Sometimes we are not so much concerned with putting a truth across as with PROVING OUR POINT; pride in knowing better *and "telling someone off." And you can be sure that if you come away feeling* pretty proud of yourself *that you put someone "in his place,"* it is time to look and see in what place you have put yourself. *It is certainly not one of* humility.

Passion Sunday (Palm Sunday), A, B, C Cycle #38

READING 1

"THE LORD IS MY HELP, THEREFORE I AM NOT DISGRACED; . . . KNOWING THAT I SHALL NOT BE PUT TO SHAME . . ." (Is. 50: 4-7).

THOUGHT

If shame is endured for God it is *easier to face,* but when endured for man it brings *feelings of disgrace.*

If you are sure of God's approval you won't be put to shame. It is what *we are not sure about* that causes us to feel uneasy and affects us the most. Oh, there are some who have made themselves *sure in their belief about evil* . . . that is . . . they have glossed over the sin and *dulled their conscience* into thinking they are doing nothing wrong. "Everybody is doing it" is the lame excuse. And after their first few pangs of shame they no longer feel any guilt. But those *first few pangs* were the clues that *should have been heeded.* In reality most shame we feel is not shame at all *for offending God.* It is a feeling of disgrace because *we made a fool of ourselves in front of others* . . . and we are concerned about what they will *think about us.* If we would not have been found out we would not have felt ashamed. If we would worry as much about *what God thinks of us* as we do *what our neighbor thinks,* we would certainly improve at a faster rate.

APPLICATION

People may think of you as a fool for being soft-spoken to someone who needs a good tongue lashing . . . for lending a helping hand to the ungrateful, . . . for taking abuse without striking back . . . for going to Mass every day . . . for speaking out against evil when others are tolerating it and indulging in it. But if you are sure in your heart that you are enduring all things for God *your conscience will be free. You will feel no disgrace. Man's ridicule will not bother you. You will have done your part knowing that you will "not be put to shame"* (v. 7).

Passion Sunday (Palm Sunday), A, B, C Cycle   #38

READING 2

"YOUR ATTITUDE MUST BE CHRIST'S . . ." (Phil. 2: 6-11).

THOUGHT

It is difficult to have an attitude like Christ's if one has *an impersonal attitude toward Him.*

When we merely just think about Christ He seems far off and impersonal to us. And for someone to come along and ask us to "be like Him" seems a little far-fetched and *beyond our ability.* "He is God! I'm a human being. He is all perfect! I'm imperfect." That seems to sum it all up in a nutshell and "tells it like it is." It is no wonder we are apt to give up before we even start with that kind of an attitude. None of us can *fully imitate what another can do.* Some are always better than the rest; they can "out-do" us. But if we *admire* them enough, we try to learn all we can about them and *attempt to do the things in the way they do.* We try to take on the same attitude but not necessarily their appearance so as to become duplicate copies. *That is impossible!*

APPLICATION

This Scripture Reading tells us our attitude *should be Christlike: mainly submitting our will to God, having charity for those in need, having good will toward all mankind, having compassion for those in sorrow, being patient under all trials, forgiving those who hurt us, and forgetting ourselves in serving God.* None of these things are beyond your ability. Your attitude can be like Christ's if you want it to be.

Passion Sunday (Palm Sunday), Cycle A #38

GOSPEL

"They Began to Say to Him One After Another, 'Surely It Is Not I, Lord?'" (Mt. 26: 14-27, 66).

Thought

A person who is *really innocent* does not have to *ask if he is guilty of something.*

What a startling announcement it would be for Jesus to suddenly make the statement *in our presence,* "One of you is about to betray me" (v. 21). We would be *so positive* that we are not the guilty one that we would ask as the disciples did, one after another "Surely, it is not I, Lord" (v. 22). We would look around at each other and *be quick to point our finger at someone else.* But ask yourself if you could *still be so positive* after reading the words of this poem.

WAS IT I, LORD?
by Mujana Darian

The Crucifixion was long ago,
And oh, how I'd like to say:
"Lord, I would not have a part,
If that happened here today."

I'd like to think . . . I'd stand right there
And suffer by Your side . . .
But . . . when I face reality,
I see my actions do not coincide.

"Was it I, Lord, who waved the palm
And loudly proclaimed your praise . . .
Yet . . . *when someone talked against You,*
No objection did I raise?"

"Was it I, Lord, who went to sleep
When You prayed there for our sake . . .
*While I let many a Mass go by
And no effort for You did I make?"*

"Was it I, Lord, who washed my hands
And condemned You to the Cross . . .
*When I showed such indifference
To my brothers and their loss?"*

"Was it I, Lord, who made Your crown
That mocked You as a king . . .
*With my woven acts of jealousy
And words that crush and sting?"*

"Was it I, Lord, who bound Your hands
And tied You to that post . . .
*When in angry words I lashed right out
Against those who loved me most?"*

"Was it I, Lord, who built Your cross
Out of heavy wooden beams . . .
*When I clung to transient pleasures
And worldly wants and schemes?"*

"Was it I, Lord, who was forced to help
And I recognized You not . . .
*When I grumbled about my fellow man
And helping him with his lot?"*

"Was it I, Lord, who placed the nails
In Your hands and Your feet . . .
*With explosive blows of anger
When I was faced with sheer defeat?"*

"Was it I, Lord, who waited there
And further proof demanded . . .
*When You answered not my prayers
In the way that I commanded?"*

"Was it I, Lord, who took Your robe
And for it cast the dice . . .
*When confronted with my religion
I always tried to compromise?"*

"Was it I, Lord, who watched You die
And saw the lightning tear the air . . .
*Blind to the fact . . . that in every deed . . .
I have most certainly done my share?"*

"Was it I, Lord, who sealed Your tomb
As a precautionary measure . . .
*When my pride and stubborn obstinacy
Built a stone wall of displeasure?"*

Yes, the Crucifixion was long ago,
But I know . . . now . . . I could not say,
"Lord, I would not have a part
If that happened here today."

"Oh, Lord, if it is not too late
In the time that is left for me . . .
In my every waking moment
Let me *prove my love for Thee.*"

"Oh, Lord, have mercy!"

Application

We may not have been physically present at the Crucifixion, but we have all played a part in betraying and crucifying our Lord. *Spend the rest of your life* proving your love *for Him and trying to make up for all your past offenses.*

Passion Sunday (Palm Sunday), Cycle B #38

GOSPEL

"SIMON OF CYRENE . . . THEY PRESSED HIM INTO SERVICE TO CARRY THE CROSS . . ." (Mk. 14: 1 — 15, 47 or 15: 1-39).

THOUGHT

It is a shame that we have to be *forced* into helping someone *before we recognize God's will in it*. But it is better than *willfully* doing something and *never recognizing God's will at all*.

Nothing that happens in our life is by *chance*. We are in a certain place at a certain time because God wills it. *He has something that He wants us to do*. On the very *smallest thing a greater thing may depend*. And like Simon, what might seem to be an annoying interruption in our plans and an unfortunate degrading thing (such as being forced to stop and help someone who seemed to be a criminal) could very well turn out to be the best opportunity that ever came into our life. Simon's whole destiny *hinged upon helping someone else*. How many times have we been forced to help our Lord share the burden of the Cross and we grumbled and were *put out* because we wanted to do something else? He had interrupted our well-laid plans so we could help someone in need. Oh, sometimes we recognized God's will in it *after we got started*, but many is the time *we did not recognize it at all*. We lost all the blessings we could have gained by our dissatisfaction.

APPLICATION

Recognizing God's will in your daily crosses will not make them any lighter to carry, but it does give a purpose to carrying them. *Instead of being annoyed at being forced to change your plans, cheerfully adapt yourself to the situation and try to see the opportunity of serving God in it. We are all looking for the best possible opportunities for the future. You have them in your hands if you just "go along" with God* regardless of what comes into your life.

Passion Sunday (Palm Sunday), Cycle C #38

GOSPEL

"Lord, ... At Your Side I Am Prepared to Face Imprisonment and Death Itself ..." (Lk. 22: 14, 23: 56).

Thought

We think we are prepared to face a lot of things ... *until the time comes to prove our words.*

Do not be so quick to *boast* about what you can do ... unless you have *already proved you can do it.* We can see how "cocksure" Peter was in boasting of his fidelity, his willingness and *strength to even face death itself for Christ.* Yet only a few hours later, *he did not have strength enough to stay awake* one hour to pray with Him. It is always easy to be valiant in *words.* We can easily say what we *would do* as long as we do not have to *prove* our words. We are quick to pass judgment on another's cowardly action when we do not really know how we would have reacted in the same situation. When put to the test we might "go to pieces" just like anyone else. And maybe even worse! And when we fail to live up to someone's expectation of us, *we rush right in without thinking,* like Peter did when he cut off the ear of the servant. We usually do some hasty, foolish thing, trying to make up for the shame of letting someone down, and often times *cause more trouble.*

Application

"Going to pieces" when some emergency confronts you only makes it harder to get the pieces back into place after it is over. Try to remain calm and learn to "take things in stride" with God. He understand and forgives your human weaknesses, your failings and faults. He expects you in your charity to try to understand these same things in others. Peter's weaknesses did not hold him back ... do not let yours do so either.

Monday of Holy Week #258

READING 1

"HE SHALL BRING FORTH JUSTICE TO THE NATIONS, NOT CRYING OUT, NOT SHOUTING, NOT MAKING HIS VOICE HEARD IN THE STREET" (Is. 42: 1-7).

THOUGHT

"Rioting" in the cause of religion does not make one's actions *spiritually right*.

Nowadays the trend is to try to bring about justice by shouting protests and rioting in the streets. And it is effective all right. In fact, so effective it leaves an aftermath of more bitterness and hatred along with the injured and dead in the streets. It sets off a chain of reaction that *wipes out all sense of reasoning and charity for one's neighbor*. Unless *God* is the basis for social righteousness, any so-called justice won in this manner *will be short-lived*. If we are going to have a peaceful world we have to start with a peaceful people. We have to be centered in God and motivated by the principles He has given to us. There are times when our duty as Christians demands we make an *appropriate rebuke against injustice*. But in doing so, our objective should be to *glorify God and to provide a good Christian example to others*.

APPLICATION

No one can hide behind the alibi that he can rightfully sin "for his religion" *to bring about social justice. When your overambitious zeal destroys the rights and property of others it becomes an injustice. Be* prayerful and peaceful *in your approach to bring about justice* . . . "not crying out, not shouting, not making his voice heard in the street" (v. 2).

Monday of Holy Week   #258

GOSPEL

"Why Was This Perfume Not Sold? It Could Have Brought Three Hundred Silver Pieces, and the Money Have Been Given to the Poor" (Jn. 12: 1-11).

Thought

Usually the people who criticize another person for his generosity are not very generous themselves.

There is something wrong with us when *another's generosity* for his Faith causes us to *criticize* him. We should be joyous about the gift and be inspired to do the same if we can. When we "go overboard" *on economy for the Church,* we blight the real spirit of our worship. In expressing love and appreciation of our loved ones on earth, we make sacrifices many times to give a gift. We get all out of proportion at times . . . "go overboard" . . . spending more money than we should. We even use money that should have been saved for something else. If we are criticized by people like Judas, it does not bother us one bit. We made our loved one happy. We are *proving our love* and that is all that matters. *We are happy too.* Those who take pride in being practical and never being "swept away by sentiment" are usually very unhappy people. They have a shriveled, stingy soul that proclaims every call upon their generosity as either *unreasonable* or *unseasonable.*

Application

If the generosity and faith that Mary showed for our Lord inspired *all the Christians of the world,* there would be no problem with the poor. They would be taken care of. *If you are going to "go overboard" with generosity what better One could there be to bestow it upon than God through the Church? Give as generously to God as you do to your loved ones.* He certainly loves you more.

Tuesday of Holy Week #259

READING 1

"Though I Thought I Had Toiled in Vain, and For Nothing, Uselessly, Spent My Strength . . ." (Is. 49: 1-6).

Thought

It is certainly better *to fail in doing something* than to *try to do nothing and be a SUCCESS.*

We all have those days when we say we must have gotten up on the wrong side of the bed. Nothing goes right. Everything we touch turns into disaster, and our attempts to right them only make things worse. In fact, we feel it would have been better if we would have stayed in bed. All that may be true. In man's eyes we were a failure. We can truthfully say *we had nothing to be proud of that day.* Now *there* is the one thing that saves the day! On that day *if anything good comes out of our actions, we know it has to be God's doing . . . and not our's.* So we will be more apt to give Him *His rightful credit.* The other days when things go fine *we take the credit.* It is good for us to have a "bad day" occasionally. It helps to remind us that we are not so self-sufficient. We can be so "puffed-up" with our accomplishments that, like a balloon that has reached its capacity for stretching, *we can go beyond our limits with PRIDE and blow up,* destroying all the good we have done.

Application

The disappointment you are suffering today could very well be God's appointment for the day. *Cheerfully accept whatever happens as God's will. You can learn from things that go wrong as well as from the things that go right. Do the best you can. Tomorrow is a new day to work for God. Getting out of bed and going to Mass will help a great deal!*

Tuesday of Holy Week #259

GOSPEL

"You Will Lay Down Your Life for Me, Will You?" (Jn. 13: 21-33, 36-38).

Thought

Intentions to sacrifice *show* one's love of God but *completion* of them *prove* one's love.

Like Peter, we have spurts of enthusiasm . . . times when we realize *we are just not doing enough* to prove our love of God. Remember all the grandiose plans and good intentions we had at the beginning of Lent? We were going to be so different this time. We were *really* going to sacrifice for God. But somehow, little by little, one by one, all our resolutions were *diluted* and *weakened* and in some cases, *given up altogether*. We are something like a pitcher who keeps winding up but never lets go of the ball. The pitcher really looks good on the mound. He looks like he could put that ball right across the plate. But unless he *completes that "wind-up" and lets go of the ball* he will never know if he can pitch a strike or not. An intention of sacrifice not carried out is not of much value *except for making you feel good about yourself when you first made it*.

Application

If you are not satisfied with your efforts of sacrifice do not be discouraged. But in these few days left in Lent, make a REAL EFFORT TO PROVE YOUR LOVE. Attend Holy Week services. Be patient with your family. Go out of your way to help someone. Patch up a quarrel. Write a letter to someone who is lonely.

Wednesday of Holy Week #260

READING 1

"THE LORD GOD HAS GIVEN ME A WELL-TRAINED TONGUE..." (Is. 50: 4-9).

THOUGHT

Some of us have "a well-trained tongue" but by its output it is evident *the Lord did not train it.*

"Boy, she talks a mile a minute!" "Once he gets the floor you can't get a word in edgewise!" These are familiar phrases that pretty well describe some people we know . . . and maybe ourselves if we want to be honest about it. I think if we took the word "I" out of the conversation, we would discover we probably would not be able to say much. Too many times we are all wrapped up in ourselves, telling our own adventures and bragging about our own deeds and families. Being sociable and contributing by our conversation is important. It is a natural expression of good relationship with people as well as with God. But if our conversation is totally self-centered with no charity and concern of others, it is just idle chatter that makes us a nuisance to society. It is more apt to get us into trouble. Words are powerful weapons. Idle gossip, spreading rumors, words of spite and hate can do more damage than the biggest bombs. This is not the type of "well-trained tongue" our Lord is talking about.

APPLICATION

He is talking about one that knows the right words to say at the right moment; *a word of comfort when someone is sorrowful, a word of joy for the depressed, a word of hope for the discouraged, a firm word of reproach for those who need correcting, an understanding word when someone tells you his troubles, a peaceful word for the angered . . . and an absence of words for someone who needs your ear.*

Wednesday of Holy Week #260

GOSPEL

"What are You Willing to Give Me If I Hand Him Over to You?" (Mt. 26: 14-25).

Thought

Many so-called "religious people" think *first* of their own *profit* and *secondly* of their *religion*. Judas was one of these. Are you?

How easily we let our religion suffer when money or reputation is concerned. Some will do anything for a price. Before you *object so strenuously that you are not one of these* . . . you would NEVER HAND-OVER JESUS . . . examine your conscience with these examples:

Was there any time when you denied or left out your religious status on an application form for fear it would influence an employer against you? *Was not Jesus handed-over for the price of a job?*

What about the extra "moon-lighting job" that left you no time for Mass? *Was not Jesus handed-over for the price of a few luxuries?*

What about the times you used your religion as a tool to make connections? *Was not Jesus being bartered to increase your opportunities?*

What about the big "shindig" until the wee hours of the morning that left you with a "hang-over," too tired and incapable of getting up for Mass? *Was not Jesus handed-over for the price of a few drinks?*

What about the times in a restaurant or in your own home when you did not say your usual meal prayers because you were embarrassed to show others you were thankful for your blessings? *Was not Jesus handed-over for the price of someone's opinion of you?*

Application

There are certain conditions that have to be met *to take care of your economic welfare. But handing over Jesus . . . selling Him out . . . or using Him should not be one of them. The moral Christian principles of our Faith should never be sacrificed or exploited for money or opportunities to get ahead.*

Holy Thursday,
Mass of the Lord's Supper, Cycle A, B, C   #40

READING 1

"THEY SHALL TAKE SOME OF ITS BLOOD AND APPLY IT TO THE TWO DOORPOSTS AND THE LINTEL OF EVERY HOUSE IN WHICH THEY PARTAKE OF THE LAMB" (Ex. 12: 1-8, 11-14).

THOUGHT

Some people do not have *confidence* in anything unless *they feel IMPORTANT while doing it.*

Marking one's house with the blood of the lamb and eating a meal *does not seem too much to do to save one's life.* But, no doubt, in those times as well as now, there were some who refused to believe that such a *simple act* could save them. Now, if you ask them to do something difficult they *might* believe. Some have to get the feeling of accomplishing something before they think it will have any effect. It is not so much to prove their great love of God as it is to *bolster up confidence in themselves.* Of course, while they are doing this, they could very well lose track of the purpose of the act. When we are all wrapped up in pride of "self-fulfillment" *it does not leave much room for God.* Pride often produces self-complacency and self-sufficiency.

APPLICATION

You do not have to feel any "self-importance" about an act to gain something from it. *It is more important to have confidence in God than yourself. Very few of us ever accomplish anything of great importance by man's standards. Yet for God,* every act you do *cheerfully, obediently, without complaint, for Him IS OF GREAT IMPORTANCE. When you go to Mass and partake in the Eucharistic Banquet it is* the most important thing you can do *and* proves your confidence *in Christ who shed His Blood for you.*

Holy Thursday,
Mass of the Lord's Supper, Cycle A, B, C   #40

READING 2

"EVERY TIME, THEN, YOU EAT THIS BREAD AND DRINK THIS CUP, YOU PROCLAIM THE DEATH OF THE LORD UNTIL HE COMES" (1 Cor. 11: 23-26).

THOUGHT

If our *hunger for spiritual food equaled that for material food* we would not have any "drop-outs" at the Eucharistic Banquet.

We know that physically without eating and drinking there can be no life. Oh, for a time we can survive without food and water but it soon takes it toll on our body. We become listless, lose weight, dehydrate, and eventually, if we do not reach the source of supply, we will die. The same thing happens to us when we cut ourselves off from spiritual food, the Holy Eucharist. The Eucharistic Table may be ever so bountifully supplied with Food, but if we merely look at it and do not partake of it, it *can do us no good*. We can survive in our Faith for awhile, but eventually we will die. Little by little we become less interested in Mass. The words of the Scriptures hold no weight . . . no meaning. The fountain of faith that once surged through us runs dry and we become *spiritually dead*. The normal appetite cycle for food is hunger, eating, satisfaction, and *then hunger again.* If only *our hunger for God would be like that!*

APPLICATION

The reception of Communion is not a compulsory act of devotion or one of obedience; it is a voluntary one. *It should never be considered* just a routine part of Mass *that has no more meaning than standing or kneeling at the appointed time. It is a time when all our thoughts should be concentrating on our Lord. We should be eagerly, humbly awaiting the uniting of His Body and Blood with ours. Reminding ourselves, telling Him over and over again,* WE NEED HIM, WE DESIRE HIM, WE WANT HIM, AND WE CANNOT LIVE WITHOUT HIM.

Holy Thursday,
Mass of the Lord's Supper, Cycle A, B, C   #40

GOSPEL

"Then You Must Wash Each Other's Feet . . ."
(Jn. 13: 1-15).

Thought

When you think a work of charity is *below your level* it points out *just how low your level of humility really is.*

The idea of washing someone's feet does not particularly appeal to us. Now the face and hands might meet with our approval but getting down on our knees seems to be a task a little *beneath our dignity*. We can talk and boast all we want about knowing, loving, and serving God, but it is all a "lot of bunk" until we prove it by *knowing, loving, and serving man*. St. Francis felt this when he met the leper on the road. He felt revulsion, nausea, fear at the sight of the man. But he knew that unless *he could* and *would* love and serve *all men* . . . not just those who are pleasant to the eye, but *all mankind in whatever condition they are* . . . unless he did this, he could not truly say that he loved God. Oh, God did not say we would find the task easy, or we would ever eagerly look forward to it, or we would not be repulsed by it. He said: "What I just did was to give you an example: as I have done, so you must do" (v. 15). And another time He said: "Whatever you do for the least of My brethren *you do for me*" (Mt. 25: 40).

Application

Christ comes in all forms of man . . . not just those who please us: the rich, the poor, the beggars in the street, the healthy, the senile, the sick, and even the lepers, and those eaten up with cancer. The lowliness of an act of charity or the physical appearance of someone should not affect your serving another. The more difficult, the more unsightly it is, the more opportunity you have to prove your love of God. There is no one MADE for doing the dirty work, but there are those who MAKE themselves while they are doing it. *And in so doing, make themselves closer to God.*

**Good Friday,
the Passion of the Lord, Cycle A, B, C** #41

READING 1

"OUR SUFFERING THAT HE ENDURED . . ." (Is. 52: 13, 53, 12).

THOUGHT

We give so much consideration to *the cost of following Jesus* that we forget about *the cost of not following Him.*

We know from the reading of the Passion all that Jesus endured for us. It fills us with sorrow. We would like to do something about making amends. But what are we really prepared to endure for Jesus? Oh, how quickly we answer: "ANYTHING!" But when we get down to the real truth, the answer for the majority of us is "NOT MUCH." A headache *sets us on edge* and everyone else around us . . . *We could have suffered in silence.* We cannot bear certain sights and sounds without showing signs of being *aggravated . . . We could have been more tolerant.* We do not want to visit or entertain someone for duty's sake (and when we are *forced* to do so, we make sure the one visited realizes what an *imposition* it is on us) . . . *we could have been more charitable.* Peculiar faults and infirmities *grate on our sensitive feelings,* so we *avoid* these people (many times they may be the very ones who put up with us while we went through various *obnoxious stages* of growing up) . . . *we could have been more patient.* When we are misunderstood, we *sulk* instead of talking the matter out . . . *we could have been less self-centered.* We get *annoyed* when someone does not agree with us . . . *we could have been more understanding.* We say we need our rest so we do not get up earlier to go to Mass everyday . . . *we could have been less lazy.* Yes, we really endure *very little* for Jesus.

APPLICATION

God does not look for great successes and demonstrations of outstanding powers from you. He looks for a humble, charitable, true faithfulness in your heart and life. God in His great mercy and love will be pleased if you just bear cheerfully and endure for His sake all the common annoyances that disturb your everyday life. *Let these things be a source of grace rather than a source of uncharitableness.*

**Good Friday,
the Passion of the Lord, Cycle A, B, C**　　　　　　　　　#41

READING 2

"Sympathize With Our Weakness . . ."
(Heb. 4: 14-16; 5: 7-9).

Thought

Knowing your own weaknesses should encourage you *to work on them* . . . not to "give in" to them!

God wants us to be *aware* of our weaknesses so that we will see *the need for improvement*. But the awareness of them does not give us an *excuse* for not doing better. When we run ourselves down, magnify our shortcomings and brood over our failures we are not being humble. *We are just feeling sorry for ourselves.* We dig a rut for ourselves and are content to wallow in self-pity and self-reproach. We use our weaknesses as our excuses for "giving up" and "giving in" to temptation. We might fool ourselves into believing it is an excuse by earthly standards, but it *sure won't hold up as an excuse for Heaven.* Nothing can disqualify us more quickly for making a success than the habit of not facing up to our weaknesses and running away from failures. Face them with a determination to "lick" them. We cannot expect improvement *if we have no desire to do better.* God knows our weaknesses better than we do. He always gives us the strength and means to overcome them. All we have to do is ASK FOR HIS HELP. St. Paul says: "I can do all things in Him who strengthens me" (Phil. 4: 13).

Application

When you are conscious of your faults and weaknesses *you are not so bad off. It is when you are* not aware of them *that matters get worse. And it is even worse when you have given up and let them "lick" you.* Taking a check on yourself at least once a week is necessary and helpful. DO NOT GLOSS ANYTHING OVER. BE HONEST WITH YOURSELF. *It will allow you to spot and remedy things before they get out of hand. And while you are conscious of your own faults, it should help you to be* more indulgent toward those of others.

Good Friday,
the Passion of the Lord, Cycle A, B, C   #41

GOSPEL

"AM I NOT TO DRINK THE CUP THE FATHER HAS GIVEN ME?" (Jn. 18: 1-19, 42).

THOUGHT

The ability to *accept and overcome* the hardships of suffering usually equals our *capacity to suffer.*

Many times we have a *choice* about certain trials. The decision to embrace them or turn away from them is entirely up to us. Then there are some trials over which we have *no choice.* They come without obtaining our approval. There is no turning away. THEY EMBRACE US in such a manner we cannot help but bear them. *God has assigned them.* They are necessary to temper us, to bring out the gem-like qualities that are hidden under our too earthly covering. *We have to drink from the cup God has given to us.* The important part then is *how we choose* to accept the cup. Are we going to act like a small child *kicking and protesting* all the time while the dose of medicine is being administered? Or like an adult, *accepting* the bitter stuff, knowing that it will be for our own good. *Everything that happens to us has to be for good or God would not let it happen.* Any assignment from God of trial or misery on earth is worth every bit of it if it ASSURES US OF HEAVEN.

APPLICATION

The hardship of suffering is sometimes felt more by those who stand by watching, taking care of the sick person's needs. The demands *made upon you may at times seem* beyond limits; *beyond your endurance.* YOU ARE FORCED TO DRINK FROM THE SAME CUP *and it isn't easy, especially when the sick person's spirit is stoical and sour. Be charitable. Be cheerful and have more patience with him. If you are enduring it anyway you might as well gain merit for it. And afterwards you will never regret the moments of having been charitable, but YOU WILL REGRET ALL THE MOMENTS OF HAVING BEEN UNCHARITABLE.*

Easter Vigil, Cycle A, B, C #42

EPISTLE

"Resurrection . . ." (Rom. 6: 3-11).

Thought

We do not need the *proof* of "Resurrection" so much as we need the *Source* of the power of resurrection.

The hired guards claimed to be asleep; the women came to anoint Jesus; Thomas doubted! With so many recorded human uncertainties the Resurrection story *could never have survived had it not been true.* Also, with so many willing to pay a *reward for proof* that Christ's Body had been removed and buried elsewhere, *greedy men would have found the Body if there was any to be found.* Those who stumble over the belief in the Resurrection of our Lord and the Real Presence of that same risen Lord in the Sacred Host of Holy Communion can learn much from the miracles of nature. Think of the hatching of the chick from the egg. All the time you were waiting, all you could see was the *outward appearance of an egg.* Man told you the chick would come forth, but there was nothing to indicate the substance had changed inside. Then things began to happen. The egg shell tombs began to crack open. Living creatures burst forth all under their own power! MAN'S WORD WAS PROVED. *If a chick hidden under the outward appearance of an egg could come forth at the appointed time,* HOW COULD ANYONE DOUBT THAT THE ONE WHO CREATED THE CHICK COULD NOT COME FORTH AT HIS APPOINTED TIME? He is God! Christ lived and died to save us. His Resurrection gives us proof of His conquering death!

Application

We do not need the proof of Resurrection so much as we need the Source. *WE NEED GOD! Enclose yourself within God, then everything must go through Him first and nothing can harm you.*

Easter Vigil, Cycle A #42

GOSPEL

"Suddenly There Was A Mighty Earthquake . . ."
(Mt. 28: 1-10).

Thought

The main reaction to an earthquake is at first *fear,* but the aftermath can be *one of many emotions* . . . despair, thankfulness, hope, sorrow, etc.

Earthquakes are always frightening. Perhaps because we have *no control over them;* they are beyond our power. We are at the mercy of the elements. And afterwards there are many mixed emotions. There was an earthquake at the Crucifixion and another at the Resurrection. In the first one, when Jesus went down into death, an all-enveloping darkness covered the earth. It seemed to "spell out" the way His friends felt inside; *utterly lost and forsaken.* There was no consolation. There was no encouraging sign. There was just a frightening mass of darkness that brought fear . . . with no hope. *For to all appearances Jesus had suffered complete failure for his cause.* Only His enemies rejoiced and felt triumphant. They felt they had been right. They had proved their case . . . *so they thought.* This Jesus was not the Son of God as he had claimed to be. At the second earthquake when Jesus arose triumphantly from the dead, a dazzling brightness poured forth. But this brightness brought no joy to His enemies; it brought terror into the hearts of the faithless. "The guards grew paralyzed with fear of him and fell down like dead men" (v. 4). But for those who were faithful, although there was still fear, there was no longer darkness. The *earlier promises* that Jesus would rise from the dead *suddenly were brought home to them.* All their hopes were fulfilled. Peace, comfort, and encouragement now reigned forever in their hearts.

Application

It is no small thing to be on terms of friendship with Jesus. *If you share His friendship, as a true friend, you are expected to share in His sufferings also. There are lots of disasters and earth-shaking trials that may and do come into your life. But no matter how dark and hopeless things might look,* if you have faith in God, *the brightness will come; you will share in His glory.*

Easter Vigil, Cycle B #42

GOSPEL

"Who Will Roll Back the Stone For Us from the Entrance to the Tomb?" (Mk. 16: 1-8).

Thought

The purpose of the stone being rolled back was *not to let Jesus out* but to *let the disciples come in.*

How to roll back that huge stone that man had placed there was, no doubt, a great concern to the women as they walked along the road toward the tomb. The ointment was already obtained to anoint Jesus. That was no problem. But that stone . . . how would they ever get that rolled back? Yes, like many of us, *they were worrying about something in the future which God in his providence had already taken care of.* How different were their thoughts as they *approached* the tomb from those they had when they left. In just a brief time their *anxiety had turned to great joy.* JESUS HAD TRULY RISEN FROM THE DEAD AS HE PROMISED! We are also filled with anxiety and even somewhat discouraged about the future when we can see no way out. But once we approach the situation, get the facts and see how things really are, our hearts become lighter; we have a glimmer of hope. Time can make a big difference in our outlook on life. The difference between failure and success can oftentimes be but a few minutes. Be patient. Use your time wisely and prudently searching for God's will in all things.

Application

Obstacles, huge stones of our weaknesses and sins, can also get in your way delaying you in your search for Jesus. *Do not let their enormous size discourage you. God is not worried or deterred by the size of things. He just wants you to LOOK FOR HIM. He takes care of all the obstacles if we really want them taken away. GO TO CONFESSION. No sin is too great for God to forgive, if you are truly sorry for it. Let this Easter be one that will influence the rest of your life.*

Easter Vigil, Cycle C #42

GOSPEL

"But the Story Seemed Like Nonsense and They Refused to Believe Them . . ." (Lk. 24: 1-12).

Thought

Jesus was *deserted* by his followers *before his death* just as He was *deserted when He had risen* . . . and is still being deserted.

After hearing the message the women had brought, one might wonder *what was the matter with those apostles* that they would think "the story seemed like nonsense and they refused to believe them" (v. 11). Did they not hear the words of Jesus when He told what was to come? Did He not speak to them of His death and resurrection? Did all the promises He made "go in one ear and out the other" . . . in the same way as when we hear the words of the Scriptures or a sermon? Oh, yes, we may feel these *remotely* concern us, but more *figuratively and allegorically than literally*. We somehow harbor the notion that there is *some other way* for us to get to Heaven; perhaps something that won't *demand so much trust and faith*. Some of us might claim WE WOULD HAVE LISTENED if we had lived then. We would not have failed to believe the message as the apostles did. What dreamers we are! We ALONE would have shown our faithfulness *when we do not always show it now!* When we are *prepared* for a test we can hold up under it fairly well. But when it comes suddenly, catches us off guard, makes an immediate demand upon our faithfulness . . . the *real test* is made. We often times find that we are not as strong as we thought we were; our failure to meet the test is revealed. NEVER BE TOO SURE OF YOURSELF.

Application

History repeats man's story of failure after failure to remain true to God. It also records repeated forgiveness. *Unfaithfulness is not a* final condition . . . *unless you let it be so.* THE RELATIONSHIP OF REPENTANCE BINDS US TO GOD. *He is willing to forgive your rebellion, your disobedience, your unfaithfulness. God is always there waiting for you to turn to Him and say, "I AM SORRY." Go to confession. Make this Easter be one of true joy.*

Easter Sunday, Cycle A, B, C #43

READING 1

"He Commissioned Us to Preach to the People and to Bear Witness . . ." (Acts 10: 34, 37-43).

Thought
Some can *fill that preaching part* all right but they sure *fall down on bearing witness to Christ.*

Peter is not telling us God wants us all suddenly to be "preachers" or to climb up on a soap box and start giving speeches about religion. He is telling us through our baptism in Christ *we have been chosen and equipped by the same Spirit as Jesus;* we are to live our life as witnesses of Christ. It is not only a privilege but our duty to do so. This does not mean we are to be *aggressive* and CRAM RELIGION DOWN EVERYONE'S THROAT, preaching at them, threatening them with the consequences of not heeding our words. If we keep *preaching at someone,* he eventually *turns us off* . . . and very well could turn God off altogether. This approach in itself is not Christ-like. It is more dictator-like, more like the Pharisees. A more convincing witness is one who *lives what he proclaims with his mouth.* We should live in a manner that makes it plain that Jesus is an ever-present source of strength and joy to us. "Bearing witness" to Christ should make you more considerate of others, more patient, more willing to sacrifice, and more cheerful and hopeful *under all circumstances.*

Application
On this joyous Easter day when your thoughts are centered on the Risen Christ and all that He has done for your salvation, you feel transformed. *You feel as though you were born anew! Even the bright colorful spring clothes and the flowers on the altar bear witness to the joy in your heart. You actually* feel more conscious of His Presence *and more inclined to bear witness, to give testimony of Him. In this wonderful mood start anew today.* Wipe off the old slate. *Mend the quarrels. Give yourself and others a new outlook on life.* Let this Easter be a resurrection of your whole way of life for God.

Easter Sunday, Cycle A, B, C   #43
READING 2

"Be Intent on Things Above Rather Than on Things of Earth" (Col. 3: 1-4).

Thought

What you feel on a mountain top is soon dissipated when you get back *down to earth.*

On this wonderful day so filled with the joy of Easter, it does not seem too difficult *to raise our thoughts to God and forget about all the problems of earth.* All creation seems to *remind us* to rise above the earth; mist and fog rise to dissipate, smoke goes up from the chimney, balloons and kites fly into the air, plants and trees reach upward, and even man himself likes to climb up above ground level. Sometimes he expends great efforts in scaling a mountain; he battles the elements of nature and endangers "life and limb" to get a better view of the world below him. *How wonderful it would be if we would expend even half that effort to obtain heavenly goals.* But just as the feeling one has on a mountain top does not last long, the exhilarating feeling of Easter does not last long either. We become more material-minded and more apt to remark: "It is easy to say to be "intent on things above" but *when you have a living to make,* a family to support, you have to keep your mind pretty much on earth if you are going to make a success of it." And it is true to some extent. That is, if one thinks he has to be *down on his knees continuously praying.* Raising your thoughts to God does not require that at all . . . but it *probably would help if you did get down on your knees once in a while.* It requires offering your whole day to God; living your life, doing your work with one goal in mind . . . eternity with God in Heaven.

Application

A routine morning offering that is quickly done and then forgotten the rest of the day *does not really* meet the requirements. *You need to remind yourself often. And when you start to get impatient, when you feel irritable, when the drudgery of work pulls you down, when you are wrongly blamed and feel like reacting in an uncharitable way, remind yourself "IS THIS WHAT I AM OFFERING TO GOD?" Then say a short prayer like "My God and my All" or "All for Thee, dear Jesus" and start again with the grace of God in your heart.*

Easter Sunday, Cycle A, B, C #43

READING 2

"Do You Not Know That A Little Yeast Has Its Effect All Through the Dough?" (1 Cor. 5: 6-8).

Thought

Yeast has an effect on almost all the ingredients, but the *results of the finished product depend upon the quality of the ingredients used.*

Anyone who has watched yeast dough rise will know that it seems like somewhat of a miracle in itself. The flour, eggs, salt, and other ingredients are just piles of inactive material; *they can do nothing by themselves.* They remain enveloped in their own characteristics and eventually decay if not used. But add the yeast, mix them all together, one sharing with the other, and almost at once things start to happen. They take on another form and rise above the things they once were. They can be punched down again and again but they continue to rise. Life is like that. *Alone we can do nothing of lasting importance.* But if we add God . . . the yeast . . . to our actions, all obstacles are overcome. Working slowly and quietly, faith transforms every part of our moral being, every capacity in us until the entire old "I" is gone; transformed into a new creation. And no matter how many falls we have, how many times we are punched down, we always have the assurance of rising again.

Application

But every good cook knows that there are times when some of the ingredients she has been using *have to be* thrown out. *They have become stale, rancid, and lost their ability* to do what they were made to do. *She knows that one inferior ingredient can spoil the whole batch. So she goes out and acquires new ingredients. Easter reminds us to start anew. Our faith can become stale and even rancid unless we have a* renewal program *from time to time.* Make this Easter your renewal. *Go to confession, attend Mass more often. Show God that if He cared enough about you to die for you, you care enough about Him TO LIVE FOR HIM.*

Easter Sunday, Cycle A, B, C #43

GOSPEL

"He Did Not Enter But Bent Down to Peer in . . ."
(Jn. 20: 1-9).

Thought

Some of us prefer to just "peer in" at our religion because it might cost us some *time and effort if we really entered into it.*

Too many times we do not really enter into our Faith. We stand on the outside, peering in as observers, never really taking part. Maybe we are afraid it might cost us too much of our free time. Or we are sort of waiting to see how things turn out before we fully commit ourselves. Oh, we have proof with our baptismal records and our mouth has already proclaimed we are Catholics, but that does not include the rest of us. *Our mind and body has not been committed to work for God.* We forget that just joining as a member of the Church won't save us. Our Church membership has obligations as well as privileges. It is not so much the amount of Sunday offerings that counts as our day-to-day participation in carrying out God's message. It is *what we do as individuals that* will qualify or disqualify us for a place in Heaven.

Application

Thousands of men and women wishing the Church well from a distance are not worth one person doing his part, lifting his burden from *within. On this wonderful Easter day filled with hope and joy of Resurrection, show your gratitude to God for all He has done for you. Make up your mind* really to partake in your church activities. *Join the parish organizations that bear the burden of the work. If you have any special talents or abilities that would be of help, offer your services to your pastor. And if some handicap prevents you from doing these things* pray for those who do the work. *LIVE YOUR LIFE FOR GOD.*

Feast of the Chair of Peter, Apostle, February 22 #535

READING 1
"God's Flock Is in Your Midst; Give It A Shepherd's Care" (1 Pt. 5: 1-4).

Thought
If a shepherd expects to get any benefit from his flock he has to *take care of his sheep.*

As in all professions, there are all kinds of shepherds with all degrees of faithfulness. The wise, conscientious ones take their responsibility seriously while the foolish ones take their's lightly. One is interested in how his care *will profit the sheep,* while the other is more interested in *how his sheep will profit him.* A shepherd's main interest is in his sheep. He knows if he does not take good care of his flock it cannot provide him with the things necessary to sustain his own life. If they are haphazardly taken care of he knows that part of them will be lost and *he will suffer from the consequences.* The same lesson applies to our association with others. Whether we are aware of it or not, we all have a responsibility toward them. *Where we lead them,* directly or indirectly, to God or away from Him, rests on our shoulders. *How we lead them* . . . charitably or uncharitably, cracking a whip or gently prodding to keep them in line, will determine our own lot. *Why we lead them,* to gain profit for ourselves or to profit them, is something for which we will have to answer.

Application
The shepherd's main implements are his rod and staff. They can be used as a prod to guide, to discipline, as a means to count his sheep, as a weapon against the enemy, and as a support to steady himself over rocky terrain. He is careful not to lay them down. He always has them within reach. GOD IS YOUR MAIN STAFF THAT WILL SUPPORT YOU THROUGH ALL PERILS. *He gave you the commandments, the Church, the priests as a rod to guide and discipline you . . . as well as for you to use for those under your care. Pay heed to them. Like the wise shepherd* allow as small a space as possible to come between your Staff . . . GOD . . . and yourself.

Feast of the Chair of Peter, Apostle, February 22 #535

GOSPEL

"On This Rock I Will Build My Church . . ." (Mt. 16: 13-19).

Thought

WE NEED GOD to *build* the Church but HE NEEDS US to *occupy it.*

There is more to building a structure than just putting a few boards or bricks together. We can make a comparison with our Faith. First, there must be a *need felt* or some purpose in building . . . a school for teaching, a bank for money, etc.; WE NEED GOD so we *have* a purpose for the building of our Faith. Then, an architect must "draw-up" the plans to have the stress in the right places; WE NEED GOD as our Architect to have the right plans. Then, the proper materials must be obtained; WE NEED GOD, his grace, his laws, his words in the Scriptures as our materials. Then come the builders . . . the carpenters, steel workers, electricians, etc. . . . to construct the building; GOD NEEDS US to carry out that part and *our way* of assembling will determine how strong it will be. And finally, the building needs the people for whom it was made; GOD NEEDS US as occupants.

Application

God said: ". . . on this rock I will build my church . . ." (v. 18), but he did not say he would FORCE you to live in it. If you want to live in your Faith *and* how long you want to live in it *are determined by your own free will. Baptism gives you the key. You can enter only as long as you keep that key unbent and free of the corrosion of sin. Of course, there is really no problem if you want to repair that key. God is the "world's greatest locksmith." Go to confession. Turn in your old key. God has plenty of duplicates.*

Feast of St. Joseph,
Husband of Mary, March 19   #543

READING 1

"I WILL RAISE UP YOUR HEIR AFTER YOU . . ."
(2 Sm. 7: 4-5, 12-14, 16).

THOUGHT

Some parents are so busy with activities *to help raise up other people's heirs* that they have *no time for their own.*

Raising up an heir these busy hectic days is certainly not an easy task. And it is even worse when both parents are busy attaining their own ambitions; *seeking their own self-fulfillment.* Oh, some may be busy with children but *not necessarily their own.* They are all wrapped up in various activities outside the home . . . Scouts, 4-H, Baseball Leagues, etc. . . . *with other people's children.* These projects are wonderful and beneficial to all involved, but they should not be pursued at the expense of *neglecting your own God-given responsibility of raising up your own heirs.* There has to be a limit; a line drawn somewhere to regulate the number of hours spent away from home. And you have to be guided by your own conscience.

APPLICATION

God did *say in the Scripture Reading today: "I will raise up your heir . . ." (v. 12), but he added the words* "AFTER YOU" . . . *which means he* expects your help. *When nerves become frayed, the housework is continuously neglected, when it is mostly "eating on the run" with regular meals seldom prepared, and a week-end camp-out takes priority over Mass, it is time to stop and check on yourself. Your* first responsibility is to God and your family. *What is the good of all your outside activities if they eventually* draw you from God?

Feast of St. Joseph,
Husband of Mary, March 19   #543

READING 2

"HOPING AGAINST HOPE, ABRAHAM BELIEVED . . ."
(Rom. 4: 13, 16-18, 22).

THOUGHT

The pessimistic person is against all hope because he *depends upon his human resources* instead of God's.

The Church was made and is still being made by men like Joseph and Abraham who hoped against hope. They were not bothered about situations that seemed hopeless. They were content to give their lives to works that, by the standards of the world, seemed to be *useless*. But they were not using human standards; they were using God's. They saw beyond the moment NOW into the far future. Their sole purpose was to obtain *what was at the end of the journey* . . . GOD. They never minded all the hardships that went on in-between. The prepared Christian cannot be "derailed." He has a one-track mind . . . God. He knows *where* he is going and *how* he is going to get there. He does not carry on if he is left on the side-track for awhile. *He does not lose hope.* He knows he will not be *deserted* by God with whom he has made his covenant.

APPLICATION

There may be times when the burden of the world around you lowers the pulse of your spiritual life and causes the breath of hope to almost die out. But why worry? Have hope. God is the authority on artificial respiration. Call on Him. Depend upon Him. He can restore your breath of life and replenish your hopes with a deeper abiding faith . . . if you really want it restored.

**Feast of St. Joseph,
Husband of Mary, March 19** #543

GOSPEL

"When Joseph Awoke He Did As the Angel of the Lord Had Directed Him . . ." (Mt. 1: 16, 18-21, 24).

Thought

If an angel told us to do something we would probably *do a lot of talking* about it but *very little acting upon it.*

Very little is known about the personal life that Joseph led. The fact that he was an upright, just man seemed to be sufficient words to describe his character. One thing is certain . . . he was *persistent in following whatever God had laid out for him to do.* He did not postpone or hesitate in order to evaluate the cost of uprooting his life. He got busy and acted at once. Now we would be a little different. We would figure out the "pros and cons" before acting. We would procrastinate. We get *inspirations* to do things but the "valley of indecision" catches many of us. One part of us strains forward to what should be done, but the other part remains entangled in self-doubt, timidity, and inertia.

Application

We seem to have persistence in reverse. *Year after year we* postpone *doing the things we felt should be done. We have inspirations and day dreams about accomplishing things for God but* we do nothing about them. *And sometimes we feel* frustrated, *as if waiting for some miracle that will accomplish them. Miracles are few and far between . . . unless you help them to happen by* getting busy as St. Joseph did. *BE PERSISTENT. Quit talking about your plans and get busy carrying them out for God.*

Feast of the Annunciation of our Lord, March 25 #545

READING 1

"Ask For a Sign from the Lord, Your God . . ." (Is. 7: 10-14).

Thought

Hesitating to "ask for a sign" is not *our* problem . . . our problem is *accepting the sign God chooses to give.*

We would not hesitate to ask for a sign from the Lord. In fact, we do it all the time. We ask the Lord for a sign when we want fair weather to go somewhere on an outing. We ask the Lord for a sign when we ask that our seriously ill loved one be made well again. We ask the Lord for a sign when we ask for special favors to be granted. Yet, we get a little upset when we are asked to show our *credentials* to God; to give a sign of our sincerity of faith and *accept whatever He gives us.* We know in our world of living today, how necessary it is to have credentials to prove our identity. We have a driver's license, credit cards, social security cards, etc. They are proof that indicates we *have met specified requirements* and can be trusted.

Application

God also asks for a sign of certain credentials as proof of your fulfilling the requirements of your Faith. *When the fair weather does not come . . . let your sign be one of cheerful acceptance. When your loved one dies . . . let your sign be one of acceptance of His will. When your favor is not granted . . . let your sign be trust in His wisdom of knowing what is good for you. It is all right to ask for a sign from God,* if you are willing to abide by the *way he answers it.*

Feast of the Annunciation of our Lord, March 25

#545

READING 2

"SACRIFICES AND OFFERINGS . . ." (Heb. 10: 4-10).

THOUGHT

Your sacrifices are not necessary *for God* but they are *for you*.

In this modern age when "self-interest" appears to be the rage, "sacrifices and offerings" for God seem to be "out of date." Things come so easily for the majority of us that some think they have *outgrown the need for God*. They either give no thought to Him at all or if they do, it is a passing glance. He has become more of a "character" in a book or a screen play to them. And as long as they are getting all they want right now, *using their own will,* they cannot see any reason for doing God's will, much less making sacrifices for Him. Such foolish, dangerous thinking! "Easy come, easy go" is a familiar term that we often use. It can also apply to God's gifts; what we misuse, we can quickly lose in one brief second of disaster.

APPLICATION

God does not want or need sacrifices from you only "offered according to the prescriptions of the law" (v. 8). He wants those coming from your heart, that you WANT TO DO out of love and gratitude *for all He has given to you. Try to do something extra special today for God. Give proof of your love by your actions.*

**Feast of the Annunciation of
our Lord, March 25**   #545

GOSPEL

"You Have Found Favor With God . . ." (Lk. 1: 26-38).

Thought

You do not have to concern yourself with *finding favor with God* if you are *always favoring Him in your actions.*

The angel tells us Mary had "found favor with God" (v. 30), but he did not mention any great earth-shaking thing that she had done to obtain it. With God as the center of her thoughts, she simply went about doing her work, living her life, trying to please Him in all her actions. Her daily routine of life did not hold her back from seeking God. Just as yours should not. Oh, our opportunity to "work-out" a plan of God's is not of the same magnitude of Mary's, but *God does have a definite life-plan for everyone of us.* It is constantly pulling at us, urging us, guiding us visibly or invisibly toward some *exact thing* that God wants us to accomplish as our purpose for living. It makes no difference how limited our abilities and resources are. That is no problem. The angel also reminds us: ". . . nothing is impossible with God" (v. 37).

Application

Ask Mary to help you submit your will to God. And then, try to the best of your ability *to carry out God's will. There are no common, ordinary, unnecessary events in your life. Each event works as a piece in a jig-saw puzzle.* One piece depends upon another, *and not until it is fitted and adjusted will it work out right to complete the picture.*

INDEX

abortion, attitude toward, 90
Abraham, 36, 154
accusations, 111, 112
achievement, 23
actions, 25, 31
Adam and Eve, 12, 13
affliction, 75
age, 93
alms, 49, 87
ambassador, 4
angel, 155, 158
anger, 59, 80, 96, 116
anguish, 27
annoyances, 63, 140
anxiety, 18, 145
apology, 66, 80
apostasy, 122
apostles, 146
appearances, 77
apprehension, 51
attitude, Christ-like, 125
beggar, 49
believing, 54, 82
betrayal, 126
blabbing everything, 56
blessings, 6, 83
blind man, the, 79
blindness, spiritual, 79
boasting, 130
changes, 90
character, 77
charity, 22, 43, 49, 118, 129, 139, 140
chip-on-your-shoulder, 72
choice, making a, 28, 142
Christian, 31, 52. 55, 72, 78, 84, 87, 131
chronic condition, 104
Church and authority, 45, 60, 152
Church member, 31, 150
Church updating, 90, 97, 121
clemency, 52

comfort, 102
commandments, 57, 69,. 70
common sense, 73, 90
Communion, 137, 138, 143
compassion, 53, 80
complaints, 114
confession, 13, 38
confidence, 137
conflicts of opinion, 96
conscience, 16, 50, 78, 80, 116, 117, 124
conversation, 135
conversion, 116
convictions, 26, 78, 116, 123
co-operation, 28
correction, 22, 71
covenant, 15, 103, 118
coward, 21, 47, 116, 123, 130
credentials, 156
credit for deeds, 5, 133
criticism, 132
crosses, 7, 126, 129
crying, 18
Crucifixion, 126, 144
curse, 6
darkness, 39, 78, 79, 86, 144
death, 100, 109, 119
deceit, 46
delusion, 44
dependence upon God, 37, 93
depraved, 94
devil, 14, 17, 20, 63, 97
disappointments, 133
disapproval, voicing, 101
disgrace, 124
dissension, 72
Divine Providence, 61, 145
doubt, 96
dress styles, 60
drinking, 6, 40
drugs, attitude about, 12, 20, 90
earth, attachment to, 88, 105

earthquake, 144
economy, 132
Elisha, 109
embarrassment, 99
emergency, 75, 130
emotion, 109
enduring for Jesus, 140
enemies, 32
enthusiasm, 134
envy, 9, 47, 50
Ephesians, 78
evil acts, 79
examples, giving, 45, 61
extraordinary things, 65
failure, 39, 86, 120, 133, 141
faith, 19, 26, 36, 54, 55, 56, 64, 76, 81, 84, 87, 97, 104, 122, 138, 149, 150
faithfulness, 146, 151
fallen away, 122
fame, 33
fasting, 3, 8
faults, 96, 141
fear, 21, 30, 51
feelings, 19, 35, 109
finish line, the, 107
flesh, dwelling on, 101
folly, 58
food, 40, 138
forgiveness, 13, 30, 68
forgotten, 92
Francis, St., 49, 58, 139
Garden of Gethsemane, 27, 130, 142
generosity, 132
gift, 81
goal, 86, 95, 107, 154
going-to-pieces, 130
good old days, 106
grace, 38
greatness, 33
grouchiness, 72, 74
grudge, 68, 96
guilt, 52, 62, 126

hardship, 34
hating life, 105
hatred, 32, 50, 105
heirs, 153
helping someone, 129
holiness, 41
hope, 95, 100, 154
hopeless, 44, 82, 94, 122, 148, 154
humble, 76
humility, 99, 123, 139
ideals, 88
illness, 75
immorality, 78, 101
impatience, 104, 114
important, feeling, 137
impression, making an, 25, 77
impulsive words, 35, 66, 74
inconveniences, 7
indecision, 155
indifference, 78
indignant, 47, 66
infirmities, 93, 104
inheritance, 53
innocent, 89, 126
inspiration, 95, 155
intentions, 134
involved, getting, 87
Israel, people of, 33, 54
jealousy, 9, 47, 50
job and duties, 23
Joseph, 50
Joseph, St., 154, 155
joy, 56
Judas, 17, 136
judgment of others, 77, 94, 111, 112
justice, 42, 131
kindness, 32
knowledge, 12, 36, 46, 97
Last Supper, 126, 138, 139
Lazarus, 102, 110
lies, 21, 46
life, 29, 158

life, immortal, 119
life-plan, 158
love, 32, 49, 57, 74, 103
Love, Divine, 82, 102
Martha and Mary, 102
Mary, 158
Mary Magdalen, 132
Mass, 84, 91, 138
Mass, missing, 16
measures, 43, 90
miracles, 110, 155
misfortunes, 37
misrepresenting facts, 46
mockery, 58
Moses, 54, 60, 94, 103
motive, 58, 74
mourn, those who, 102
name, 33
nation, our, 67
needs, 18
needs, providing for, 83
neighbor, 49, 74, 111
novenas, 24
obedience, 104
objection, 9, 116
obnoxious, 96
offering, morning, 148
offering, Sunday, 150
opportunity, 28, 47, 83, 129
over-indulgence, 6, 40
parents, 69, 70, 83, 153
Passion, Christ's, 126, 140
past, the, 13, 106, 112
patience, 114
patriotism, 67
Paul, St., 37, 58, 78, 101, 107, 141
perseverance, 23, 90, 155
pessimistic person, 154
Peter, St., 17, 35, 41, 130, 134, 147
Pharisees, 9, 72, 76, 91, 99, 147
planning, 90
plotting evil, 98

Pope, 121
possession, 88, 105
prayer, 24, 29, 41, 76, 94, 122
prejudice, 121
presumption, 20
pretense, 64
pride, 29, 47, 50, 60, 71, 76, 123, 133, 137
priest, 45
Prodigal son, 53
promise, 15
Promised Land, 54
proof, 26, 54, 143
proving our point, 123
prudence, 73
punishment, 21, 48, 58
quarrels, 50
questions, 108
rebellion, 90
rebuke, 89
religion, 58, 91, 116, 136, 147, 150
religious act, 5
repentance, 11
reproof, 89
responsibility, 87, 154
Resurrection, 143, 144. 146
revenge, 50, 98
reverence in Church, 60
reward, 48
ridicule, 124
rioting, 131
risks, 20
rumors, 111
Sabbath, 91
Sacrifice, 3, 8, 9, 36, 132, 134, 157
Samaritan woman, 56, 64
Scriptures, interpreting the, 121
Scriptures, listening to the, 146
self-complacency, 62
self-discipline, 40
self-fulfillment, 10, 153
self-interest, 115, 157

selfishness, 87
self-pity, 27, 29, 85, 120, 141
senses, pleasing the, 40
setting things right, 44
Shadrach, Meshach, and Abednego, 116
shame, 124
share, 34, 53
shepherd, 151
sign, a, 26, 156
silence, 47, 71, 78, 87
Simon of Cyrene, 129
sin, 13, 38, 44, 62, 76, 78, 79, 82, 112, 124
sinner, return of, 11, 54, 122
sins of omission, 22, 49
slander, 111
slave, a, 85, 117
smoking, 40
social justice, 131
standard of living, 67
stick-to-itiveness, 97
success, 90, 120
suffering, 92, 140, 142
sympathy, 102
talents, 115
taken in, 99, 100
tax collector, 11, 76
teaching and practice, 45

temper, 59
temperance, 40
temptation, 6, 14, 17, 20, 117
test, 17, 36, 146
testimony, giving, 113
things, big and little, 63, 65
time, 28, 145
tomb, the, 145
tongue, 111, 135
tragedy, 62
Transfiguration, 38, 41
trials, 142
trouble, 39
truth, 21, 113, 116, 117, 123
uncharitableness, 53, 140, 142
unkindly acts, 52
unworthiness, 41, 82, 93
virtuous deeds, 29
weaknesses, 141
will, God's and man's, 4, 129, 158
wisdom, 12, 73
witness, 113, 147
words, 19, 46, 135
work, 85
worry, 13, 18, 55, 154
yeast, 104, 150
zeal, 59, 122, 131